Navigation for Walkers

BY JULIAN TIPPETT

Navigation for Walkers 1st edition 2001.

Published by Cordee, 3a DeMontfort Street, Leicester LE1 7HD. www.cordee.co.uk

Copyright © Julian Tippett 2001.

ISBN 1 871890 54 3

Photography by Julian Tippett; John Dawson, Paul Milligan and Gordon Gadsby.

Design Mike Dunmore. Colour repro Prestige Filmsetters, Leicester.
Printed by Fratelli Spada SpA, Rome.

Ordnance Survey®

This product includes mapping data licensed from Ordnance Survey with the permission of the Controller of Her Majesty's Stationary Office © copyright. All rights reserved Licence No 43456U.

HARVEY

This product contains maps reproduced with the permission of
Harvey, 12-16 Main Street, Doune FK16 6BJ. www.harveymaps.co.uk

Disclaimer. While every attempt has been made to ensure that the instructions in this book cover the subject safely and in full detail, the author and publisher cannot accept any responsibility for any accident, injury, loss or damage sustained while following any of the techniques described.

CONTENTS

Navigation for Walkers

"View from Black Crag Cumbria." Photo Gordon Gadsby

INTRODUCTION

"Footpath furniture."

The two best map series for walkers – Explorer and Outdoor Leisure. Between them they cover the whole of England, Wales and Scotland.

For millions of people there's no better leisure activity than to 'take a good walk in the country'. But what this means in practical terms can vary enormously as a five mile stroll through the autumn leaves of a wood in Surrey is a totally different proposition from tackling a strenuous route over a string of mist-shrouded Lakeland fells. Even so, whatever the type of walking, one factor stays the same – you have to find the way. Indeed, you can't enjoy the walk unless you can follow a route easily and competently; hence the plethora of walking guide-books to be seen crowding the shelves of every bookshop. Half the people you meet on a walk seems to be clutching one, for there's no doubt these books are very effective in helping people to get out on footpaths with the minimum of fuss. But they have their limitations.

To add an extra dimension to your walking why not consider the obvious alternative and learn to use a map? With one of the latest Ordnance Survey Explorer or Outdoor Leisure maps you can choose walks from any footpath, the little-used ones as well as those well-tramped, taking you into places not yet reached by the guide-book writers. Each walk you design can meet just the needs of the moment – its length, how much climbing, views, special places to visit, even to organising a foaming pint of beer at the end if you like. On the walk itself, route-finding by map is more certain, quicker and more fun than by guide-book, and you always have the option to change your plans as you go according to mood or the weather.

Whilst navigating by map takes some effort to learn, most people can become thoroughly competent map navigators if they try, which is where this volume comes in. The book goes step by step through the essentials of navigating by map taken to a standard high enough to find the way confidently in areas where the path network is well-defined on the ground. Thus you should be able to walk with ease in the most popular walking areas of the UK, and in the countryside within easy reach of cities.

The book is packed with hints and tips won over a lifetime of practical experience. An introduction to the more advanced techniques necessary for hill and moorland navigation in poor visibility is included, enough to get you started with this kind of route finding.

As a very practical subject, map reading will never be learnt just from books. Competence comes only after lots of practice, when the techniques and methods become as second nature to perform. Try to get out with your map on a walk as soon as you can and thereafter intersperse dipping into more and more of the book with practice walks out in the countryside. By taking care to choose well trodden paths for these early trials, you will be able to complete the routes successfully whilst building up knowledge and skill. See the margin notes on page 10 for a list of the essential items of equipment you will need.

In the UK, the start of the 21st century is a particularly good time to begin map reading. The Ordnance Survey (OS), the premier UK mapping agency, is well on the way to completing a reorganisation of its map series with the walker particularly in mind.

The best scale (this term is explained in chapter one) of mapping for most walking is 1:25,000. The OS has recently settled on a very clear and comprehensive set of symbols for its mapping at this scale, printed for the first time in full colour. A highly effective layout of map sheets has been devised, covering the whole of England, Wales and Scotland, and the complete set of these Explorer and Outdoor Leisure maps will have been published by 2003. Already in their short life they have come to be regarded as the standard maps for walkers to use; consequently this book is based primarily on them.

Some examples will be drawn also from 1:50,000 Landranger maps to allow readers to see that they can be used by walkers for finding the way if a 1:25,000 map is not available. These maps come into their own when planning walks, and for cycling and driving on country roads.

The rolling hills and hedged fields of lowland Britain contain most of the country's paths and see most of the walkers. Consequently all chapters in this book except one are devoted to the skills of map reading in what might be called 'easy' countryside. In the penultimate chapter we venture into moorland and hills.

Maps for walkers

Maps from the Ordnance Survey at a scale of 1:25,000:

Outdoor Leisure maps, up to fifty yellow-jacketed sheets covering the National Parks and major areas of outstanding natural beauty.

Explorer maps, about 300 orange-jacketed sheets being progressively introduced to cover all other areas. They are replacing the green Pathfinder maps.

Where in the text reference is made to Explorer maps, take it to include Outdoor Leisure as well.

Maps from the Ordnance Survey at a scale of 1:50,000:

Landranger maps, 204 magenta-jacketed sheets. An all-purpose map that shows footpaths in less detail than at 1:25,000, and is useful for driving and cycling on country roads.

Maps from Harvey Maps at 1:25,000 and 1:40,000:

About 60 sheets covering mainly popular northern wild country areas, with very clear mapping styled on orienteering maps, ideal for walkers.

"Descending from Sheffield Pike to Ullswater in the Lake District." Photo Gordon Gadsby

Equipment you will need

Map of the area of your walk
Look at the index on the back of a possible map in the bookshop to choose the one that covers your walk. Confirm you can see the whole walk in the map itself before buying. To be sure of getting the right map of a distant part of the country ring the OS helpline (See Appendix 1) to order the latest national map index (free).

Mapcase
Unless you are sure the map case is rainproof (many are not) also carry a polythene bag to enclose the map within the case during a downpour.

Compass
See advice on choosing a compass opposite.

Watch
To be sure of getting home in time.

Magnifying Glass
Or other arrangement if your eyes need help examining the fine detail of the map.

Other items are mentioned in the text.

The success of this book will be judged by the number of people introduced to the delights of doing their walks by map. But there is a higher aspiration for the budding map reader than just to learn this practical skill. This is to join the ranks of those fortunate persons who become so familiar and at ease with maps that they can read them just like a book. Such people are to be found sitting at home already enjoying the walks they will be doing on their next holiday, or making informed judgements about the history of places and the origins of the landscape. Such country lovers would no more do without maps than would an artist go without brushes and paints.

Choosing a compass

A visit to any outdoor shop quickly reveals a wide range of compasses to choose from, varying from cheap oriental offerings to expensive sighting compasses. The points to look for are:

● For a first purchase, a 'baseplate' compass similar to the one in the photos in this book is best. The ones with mirrors and special sighting arrangements are for expert use.

● Make certain it has the basic parts of rectangular baseplate and circular rotatable housing. The longer the baseplate the better; the very short ones can be frustrating when trying to take longish legs off the map.

● Distance scales for 1:25,000 and 1:50,000 (and/or romers at these scales) are useful but not essential. Other features like magnifier and marking holes are a matter of taste.

● If you want a clip-on compass you'll have to order a Silva Type 19. The advantages of this type of compass are outlined on page 44.

● European or American manufacture seems to give the best quality.

"The paths in West Sussex are defined by an oak signpost at each junction."

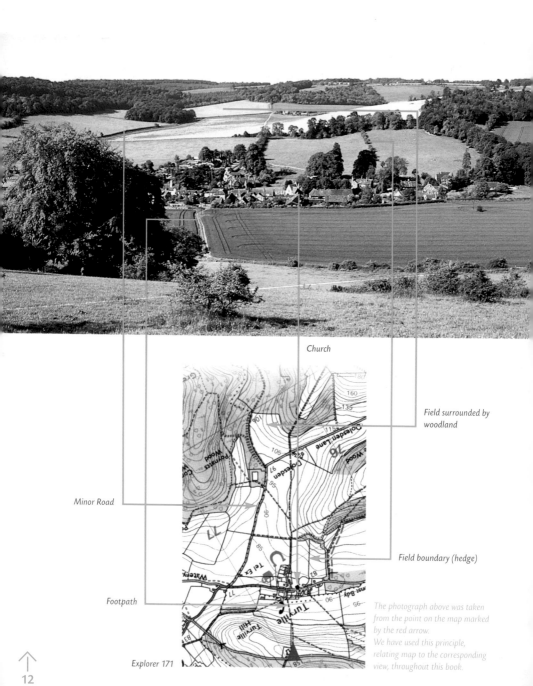

Church

Field surrounded by
woodland

Minor Road

Field boundary (hedge)

Footpath

*The photograph above was taken
from the point on the map marked
by the red arrow.
We have used this principle,
relating map to the corresponding
view, throughout this book.*

Explorer 171

The photograph (left) taken from above the village of Turville in the Chilterns represents the walker's eye-level view. Compare it with the bird's eye view of the map of the same area. (Do not be alarmed that this has been twisted round; by aligning the map to the countryside comparisons are made easier).

Notice how in the eye-level (photo) view :

• The size of the foreground is exaggerated compared with distant features.
• Part of the view can be obscured, as by the tree on the left and the white hill centre right.

Follow the blue lines to see how some common features are indicated on the map, and also start comparing map with countryside, the bread and butter of map reading. See if you can identify other features in the photograph on the map.

The curved brown lines are contours, which we look at in the next chapter.

Roads and Tracks

Extract from the key to an Explorer or Outdoor Leisure map

M I or A 6(M)	**Motorway**
A 31(T) or A 35	**Trunk or Main road**
B 3074	**Secondary road**
A 35	**Dual carriageway**
	Road generally more than 4m wide
	Road generally less than 4m wide
	Other road, drive or track, fenced and unfenced .

Put simply a map is a plan of the ground on paper – a bird's eye view; but unlike an aerial photograph which shows everything that is visible, the map is selective in what it portrays. The mapmaker chooses a small number of objects likely to be of most interest to the reader, like footpaths or streams, and shows their precise location by placing symbols in their correct places on the map. These symbols, sometimes called conventional signs, are the mapmaker's shorthand. For the sake of clarity, symbols are often printed larger than if shown at their correct relative size allowing for the reduction in scale of the map, and roads are also proportionately wider than in real life.

The margin of each map contains a key which lists and explains every class of object shown on the map, together with its symbol. The key also has much other useful information. As you get started with map reading you should take time every so often to examine the key to your own map in some detail, to learn the less frequently used symbols and to understand the other information that's there.

We now look at the more important symbols used in OS Outdoor Leisure and Explorer maps.

Roads and tracks

The roads marked in colour make up the national road network and are thus always surfaced and, apart from motorways, open to all traffic including walkers. Main roads may not be much fun to walk along, but you can include them in your walk. Some minor roads in quieter backwaters can be lovely for a stroll. A feature that sometimes comes in handy to tell where you are on the map is that each side of the road is shown with a solid or broken line, depending on whether it is fenced (or walled or hedged) or not.

*Ascending the scale of interest to walkers are **other roads**, often known as **white roads**, which could be anything from the tarmaced* drive to a private hall, to an ancient green lane or packhorse road. Since they are often wonderful to walk on in their own right, or they can connect up with other fine footpaths, it's a pity that you cannot always tell from the map whether you may include them in your walks.

With some the position is clear, in that they are minor public roads ('unclassified county roads') marked by green dots on the map, and you have every right to walk along these. All others (without green dots) are private, but often walkers are tolerated on these. Alas the only sure way of telling if you may use such a road comes on the walk itself – if you see a 'private' sign you know you're not welcome. As a precaution it helps to have an alternative route up your sleeve for such eventualities.

Footpaths

In England and Wales, you will mostly find yourself following official public paths (**Rights of Way – ROW**), shown as short green dashes for a footpath and long ones for a bridleway. Footpaths are for walkers only to use, but walkers as well as horse riders and cyclists may follow bridleways. These green dashed lines (red on a Landranger map) are copied by the OS from the **definitive map**, the official record of all ROW held by the local highway authority for its own area.

Usually ROW are walkable, with stiles provided to cross field boundaries and often a clear line of trampled ground to follow. But this is not always the case. ROW might be little-used or even blocked. One clue the map gives to their status is a thin black dashed line (**Path** in the key) accompanying the green dashed line. The black dashed line represents a path physically present on the ground.

Having two colours of dashed line for footpaths gives rise to three situations:

- **Both green and black lines are present**.
You can be confident that the ROW is walkable on the ground. If the green and black paths take slightly divergent routes, the black path usually shows the precise line to take.

White roads are often wonderful to walk.

This track leads easily to the northern cliffs of Plynlimon in central Wales. The track has double dashed lines to show it is unfenced on both sides.

Footpaths

More extracts from the key to maps at a scale of 1:25,000. Explanatory text has been omitted.

A path using the black dashed line indicates a path physically present on the ground; it is a ROW only if a green line is present too.

The **byway open to all traffic** and **road used as a public path** are special sorts of ROW. Walkers can think of them as bridleways.

In Scotland the ROW system is much less highly developed and the few ROW paths that exist are not shown as such on Ordnance Survey maps. All paths are depicted as the black dashed 'Path' in the key.

```
--------------------     Path
```

PUBLIC RIGHTS OF WAY
(Rights of way are not shown on maps of Scotland)

-------------	Footpath
— — — —	Bridleway
+–+–+–+–+	Byway open to all traffic
⊣–⊣–⊣–⊣	Road used as a public path
● ● ●	Other routes with public access

Unfenced white road

Explorer 213

Summit of Sail

The visible left hand path leads up to this saddle. From there a path ascends to Sail

The right hand invisible path crosses steep ground at the foot of cliffs

Paths split at this point

Outdoor Leisure 4

On the ascent to Sail the map shows that the path we are following (marked by green dashes) splits shortly.

The path to the right, showing a green ROW, wanders across very steep ground at the foot of the cliffs with no trace on the ground, and clearly is not a practicable route to take, although you do have a right to try it.

But the easiesr option is to go left, following the black dashed line indicating a path on the ground.

Rules for using Rights of Way and Access Land

You are happily following a grassy path, when in the field ahead you see a bull grazing freely. What should you do? In fact if it is of a beef breed and is accompanied by cows, then it is safe to proceed. A little further on, the line of the path is blocked by growing wheat. What now? You have the options of walking on the line of the path across the crop or of treating it as an obstruction and walking around the edge of the field.

These are just some of the problems you could face. The Countryside Agency (See Appendix 1) will be happy to post you free of charge its booklet "Out in the Country", which explains your rights and responsibilities.

- **Green ROW line is present but no black line.**

The path could still be perfectly well walkable, particularly if the footpaths in the district are heavily used. But this situation rings warning bells as there might well then be no path on the ground. Even if there is no path on the ground, you still have the legal right to walk the line of the ROW, although this might mean having to make your way over open country, tackling obstacles as you come to them. If you do make this choice be sure your map reading is good enough to guarantee you are on the correct line!

- **Black line exists but no green line.**

These paths are not public (unless they have green dots on their line, indicating a yet another sort of ROW). The question then comes, can you walk this path? Often such paths are fine old drove roads or quarry tracks. The situation with these is identical to white roads – see above.

Permitted paths

Take note of these paths, shown on the maps in orange. Although few in number they frequently fill missing links in the ROW network, or they lead to special places and good views. Public use of these paths has been negotiated with local landowners by the National Park or highway authority.

Waymarking

The highway authorities have a duty to waymark ROW, which they now do mostly to a high standard. Where a ROW leaves a metalled road there should be a sign post marking its start, whilst along the footpath itself, arrows are used to point the way where necessary, yellow for footpaths and blue for bridleways. The other two tell-tale signs are the presence of stiles, and a trampled line on the ground.

Access land

It is always a joy to walk over wild uncultivated land, even if we still keep to footpaths. But the chance, when it comes, to wander at will adds a wonderful extra piquancy to the event.

*At present the legal **freedom to roam**, as it is called, is confined to these categories of land, which you can look up on the key to a map:*

- *most National Trust land*
- *Forest Commission woodland*
- *National Park access land*
- *other access land.*

*Besides this legal freedom to roam there are large areas of wild land, mostly uplands, where there is **de facto** access, there to be enjoyed when you recognise it to exist. The case in Scotland is similar, where it is assumed that responsible walkers may walk unhindered on any unfenced uncultivated land. The main convention that limits this freedom is to contact estates during the deer stalking season to avoid a clash with hunting parties.*

On going to press we can expect the situation to evolve as freedom to roam legislation is enacted. The OS will be consulting widely to be sure the best way is found to depict different categories of ground on which access is permitted, and the mapping conventions for access and ROW will be adjusted accordingly.

Woods

Map readers have always nurtured a love-hate relationship with woods, depending on whether they stand outside them or inside. From afar in open country they can provide an excellent check of position because no two woods have the same shape and it is usually easy to compare the wood you can see to its counterpart on the map, to reveal exactly where you are. Woods do, of course, get felled and new ones are planted. Luckily, the pace of forestry activity is slow enough for inaccuracies to be rare in the normal life of a map. However woods, or more

Despite lacking field boundaries and other detail, Landranger maps can still be used to navigate.

There is no sign of a footpath beyond the stile, so where does it go? The map shows you must make a bee-line for the barn to the right of the small wood.

Waymarking

A yellow arrow points the way along a footpath.

Below a signpost marks the start of a public footpath.

Landranger 194

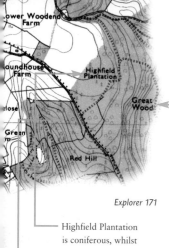

Explorer 171

Highfield Plantation
is coniferous, whilst
Great Wood is deciduous.
The wood to the south west of
Highfield Plantation is mixed.
The boundary of Highfield
Plantation is unfenced.

1:25,000 maps have other
vegetation markings (see the key).

particularly forests, are places where it is easy to lose the way.
Once inside a wood, visibility is instantly reduced and other difficulties
emerge. You can see more, or perhaps fewer, paths and forestry
tracks on the ground than are marked on the map. Unless there is good
path waymarking, these are circumstances to confound even the most
experienced navigator. Careful contour interpretation is needed then
and, as we shall see in Chapter 6, the compass might be our saviour.

Woods are shown in green with coniferous or non-coniferous tree
shape overprinting. The boundary of a wood is shown fenced or
unfenced, as with roads. On Explorer maps, additional vegetation
markings are used, as you will see in the key.

Buildings

As you can see from the key of your map, some special buildings have
their own unique symbols, like churches and windmills. But of more use
to the walker is the everyday building, a barn, a farmhouse or isolated
building. These are frequently encountered on a walk and provide
a useful check on your position. It is worth the effort to practice
comparing buildings on ground and map until you are familiar with
them. Beware one quirk: on 1:25,000 mapping a barn is shown as a
small rectangle, but a small walled animal enclosure would show up the
same on the map.

Rivers and streams

Streams are a frequently encountered feature which give good check of
position. They also help with contour interpretation by marking the
bottoms of valleys. A stream is shown as a single blue line with
a thickness proportional to its width. If greater than 8 metres in width,
the watercourse becomes a double blue line with light blue infill.
A footbridge (FB) or stepping stones are shown if present.
(On Landranger maps footbridges are shown only where they cross
double line watercourses, leaving you to guess whether a bridge exists

where a path crosses a single line stream. In popular walking areas you can expect this to be so, but elsewhere you will have to check a 1:25,000 map to be sure.)

Triangulation pillars

These concrete or stone 4-sided pillars, more commonly known as 'trig. points', are familiar sights on the summits of many of Britain's hills, marked on maps by a blue triangle. The bronze plate in the top was used by surveyors to locate their theodolites accurately.

Nowadays the OS uses satellite position fixing, making trig. points redundant. But they are pretty substantial objects which will delight us for years to come, and provide a good check in mist that we really have reached the summit.

Field boundaries

A big advantage of 1:25,000 mapping over Landranger maps is that it shows field boundaries, the thin solid black lines that criss cross the maps. Curiously, field boundaries do not figure in the map key. The lines on the map merely state that a boundary is (or was) present, there being no indication as to whether it is a wall, hedge or fence. In woods or perhaps on a moor it might be merely an earth bank.

With changing land use hedges are grubbed up, walls fall down and new fences are erected. The map makers have quite a job in keeping up with the changes, so often the markings on the map are somewhat out of date. But for all these difficulties, field boundaries remain one of the most useful navigational features of 1:25,000 mapping.

With a little practice and a healthy dose of scepticism, you will quickly be able to make sense of the boundaries as you walk. The ones you can see are usually easy to recognise on the map from their idiosyncratic kinks and bends, thus making it a relatively simple matter to allow for the ones that are missing or newly built.

Please refer to the map key for the meaning of other symbols.

Not all trig. points are located on mountain summits, although Skiddaw towering over this scene from the skyline is graced by one.

Notice the patchwork of field boundaries in the map extract, some of them bordered by drainage ditches in blue.

Outdoor Leisure 4

Outdoor Leisure 19

Can you work out which field boundaries have been removed since the map was surveyed last? Also can you follow the line the path takes in relation to the walls in the photograph?

Start the process by locating on the map the field leading down from the hill (it's the one with ring contours on it).

Now look for walls adjoining this field on both photo and map.

Contour lines, grid lines and boundaries

Besides symbols, the map is criss crossed by a number of very useful imaginary lines; that is, lines present on the map but not visible on the ground.

Contours are the curled orange or brown lines, often numbered with their height in metres above sea level. From them, you can interpret the rise and fall of the ground as will be revealed in Chapter 2.

Grid Lines make up the evenly spaced matrix of vertical and horizontal blue lines. We look at them shortly.

Administrative Boundaries are of interest to walkers merely to recognise them for what they are and then to leave them well alone. There are tales of people getting into fearful difficulties crashing through field and hedge, trying to follow boundaries that they have mistaken on the map for paths.

Other information

Each Ordnance Survey map carries a considerable amount of more or less useful information, which becomes apparent when you inspect each part of the map. The map key has been mentioned, particularly for symbols. The key contains other information of which the following is of interest to walkers: 'grid reference system', 'north points' (dealt with in Chapter 6) and 'tourist information'.

The year of publication printed in the bottom left hand corner of

BOUNDARIES

Administrative boundaries as notified to November 1997

— · — · — · —   County

— — — — —   Unitary Authority, Metropolitan District, London Borough or District

· · · · · · · · · · · · ·   Civil Parish or Community

— — — — — — —   Constituency (County, Borough, Burgh or European Assembly)

National Park Boundary

Forest Park Boundary

Scale
Explorer and Landranger Maps

These extracts show mapping of the same area at the two scales. The grid square of the Explorer map spans 4 cm, twice that of the Landranger. Thus the larger scale map has four times the area in which to show detail on the ground.

Note the 100 m divisions of the grid squares on the edge of an Explorer map, useful for estimating short distances.

Explorer 182

Landranger 166

the map, is important. From the moment a map is surveyed it starts to get out of date. Landowners grub up hedges, paths are rerouted, woods are felled and planted, and pubs, sadly, go out of business.

A recent phenomenon is to be walking happily across what you think is plain open country, only to come across a new golf course. Even so, it is rare for the changes to occur so rapidly for a map not to be usable for 10 or more years. When out walking, you must always bear in mind the possibility of the map being out of date. Though if you do discover a mismatch between map and ground, there is normally enough detail nearby that has not changed to give a solid basis for navigation.

Scale

It is now time for scale to be examined in some detail. What exactly does it mean and what is its relevance to us as walkers? Explorer and Outdoor Leisure maps have a scale 1:25,000, twice that of Landranger maps at 1:50,000. A scale of 1:25,000 means that 1 centimetre (or 1 inch, or one 'anything') on the Explorer map represents 25,000 centimetres (or inches, or 'anythings') on the ground. Thus the relationships for Landranger and Explorer shown right are true.

The blue grid squares, **always one kilometre across on the ground**, span 4cm and 2cm on Explorer and Landranger maps, respectively.

The significance of these calculations is to give the ability to estimate distances on the ground from measurements on the map, and vice versa. Thus if we measure a new walk from the Explorer map as 44cm long, we can work out that it represents 11km of real walking on the ground, a starting point for deciding whether it is what we want on the day. Similarly, measurement of shorter distances can help with navigation during the walk, as we shall see later.

The extra convenience of Explorer maps for walkers has a price. As the map extracts left show, the same amount of Explorer mapping covers only a quarter the ground covered by the equivalent Landranger, which means having to buy more maps to work at this scale. There are

Landranger

On ground		On map
50,000 cm	=	1 cm
500 m	=	1 cm
1 km	=	2 cm
1 mile	=	$1^1/_4$ inch

Explorer

On ground		On map
25,000 cm	=	1 cm
250m	=	1 cm
1 km	=	4 cm
1 mile	=	$2^1/_2$ inch

Metric v Imperial

OS maps, like most others, are now based on metric units, so this book will deal only in metres and kilometres. However, imperial diehards will be relieved to know that calculations can be done almost as well in imperial units:

Explorer $2^1/_2$ inches to one mile; Landranger $1^1/_4$ inches to 1 mile. The following conversions are accurate enough for all practical purposes:

1.6 km = 1 mile
5 km = 3 miles
100 metres = 300 feet
300 metres = 1000 feet

Some people seem to be able to mix metric with imperial according to audience and mood, but if you are looking for the simple life it is perhaps best to stick with metric.

some 400 Outdoor Leisure and Explorer sheets covering England, Wales and Scotland, many of them printed on two sides, compared with just 204 single-sided Landranger maps.

Points of the compass

When navigating we need to know the direction to walk or the direction of a distant object. Often this is best done by talking of 'lefts' and 'rights', but at other times the direction in relation to north is best. The diagram shows the points of the compass and the principal directions expressed as degrees.

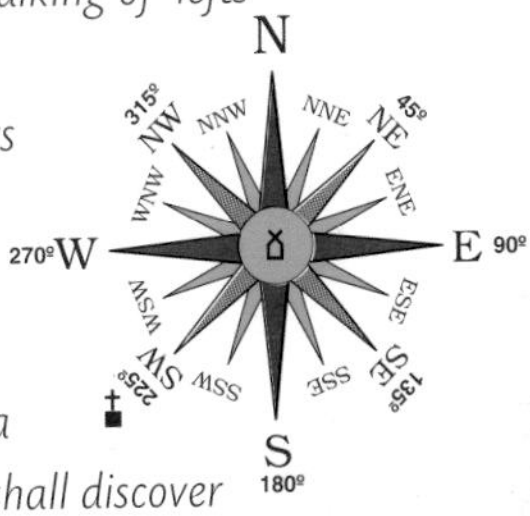

The church lies south west of the windmill (placed at the centre of the compass rose) at a bearing of 225 degrees from north. Later we shall discover that there are different sorts of north, but that need not trouble us now.

Grid References

We need now to look more closely at the blue grid of kilometre-wide squares that stretches across our maps. This has three important uses for walkers. It provides:

- a means for giving the position of a feature by a grid reference.
- the north direction for taking compass bearings.
- a convenient scale for measuring distance.

A grid reference is a number, taken from the grid, to define precisely the location of a given point, perhaps a rendezvous or a youth hostel or even the site of an accident. Knowing how to give and read grid references is not of any direct use in planning and navigating walks by maps, but it is commonly used to define a location to inform others, something walkers should be able to do. Yearbooks of the Youth Hostels Association, Ramblers' Association and the National Trust locate their properties by grid reference.

The grid covers the whole of Britain, stretching east and north from

an origin to the south-west of the Scilly Isles. See the diagram opposite showing the national grid divided into the 100km squares.
Numerical 4- and 6- figure grid references define a unique point within any of these squares. The use of the 2-letter code of the square is explained later.

 To obtain a numerical grid reference see the map extract opposite, portraying an attractive part of remote Welsh border country.
The numbering (in blue) of the vertical grid lines increases to the east, these are termed 'Eastings'. Similarly, the numbering of the horizontal lines increases to the north, 'Northings'. For ease of reading, the line numbering is repeated in the body of the map at 10km intervals, as in this extract, as well as at the edge of the map.

You wish to specify the grid reference of the village of Llangunllo (the 4-figure reference of the square it lies within is all you need for this) and, more precisely, the 6-figure reference of the cross-roads just to the north of the village (by the numbers '253' printed in black on the map).

Step 1. Identify the 1 km square containing the village.
Do this by selecting its left and bottom sides (imagine the letter 'L' that bounds the square). Take the line numbers for these two sides (downstroke of the 'L' first, just as you would write it).
This gives '**Grid square 2171**'.
 This is the 4-figure grid reference and it defines a square 1km across, quite accurate enough to locate a place such as a village.

Step 2. Now an extra figure must be added to each pair of numbers to specify to the nearest 100m where the cross-roads lies within the square. Estimate the number of tenths of the square (100m each) the cross-roads lie from 'our' two sides, once again starting with the downstroke. How far from the downstroke? **3 tenths**. How far up from the horizontal stroke? **9 tenths**. Note that you are now identifying the 100m square containing the cross-roads.

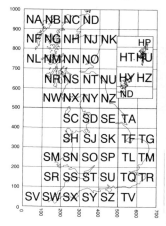

National Grid of Britain

Spend a little while relating the map to the photograph of countryside around Llangunllo using the marked features as clues. In this case the clearly identifiable features lie only in the near and middle distance.

Step 1
Specifying the 4-figure Grid Reference of Llangunllo village.
GR 2171.

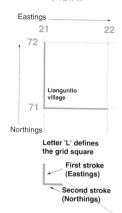

Letter 'L' defines the grid square

First stroke (Eastings)

Second stroke (Northings)

Wood

Wood

Upper Weston

Landranger 148

Step 2
*Specifying the 6-figure Grid Reference
of the cross-roads.*
GR 213 719.

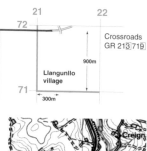

Romer

*Place the corner of the romer on the
point you are giving the grid
reference for (e.g. cross-roads), then
read from where the grid lines
intersect (taking the lower figure on
the romer)*

how many tenths north here:
and tenths east here:

Thus the 6-figure grid reference is: **'GR 213 719'.**

Step 3. When quoting a grid reference, for confirmation and as a protection against misreading, always say what the GR refers to: **'the cross-roads at GR 213 719'.**

Step 4. As seen above, each numerical reference is repeated in every 100km square. This could lead to confusion if there were uncertainty as to which square is being referred to. You can define the GR uniquely within the UK by either of two ways:

Method 1. The 'official' way adds the two-letter code allocated to the 100km square containing the grid reference, which you can find from the Grid Reference information in the map key. In this example the code is 'SO', so the full grid reference is: **'the cross-roads at GR SO 213719'**

Method 2. A more informal but commonly used way of giving a nationally unique grid reference is to quote the Landranger map sheet number containing the location. Both the YHA and the Ramblers' Association favour this method in their year books eg: **'the cross-roads at GR Map148/213719'.**

The reverse of the above procedure is needed if you are given a 6-figure grid reference which needs to be decoded to locate a particular point. Use the first, second, fourth and fifth digits of the grid reference to locate the grid square; then use the third and sixth digits to locate the point within the square, estimating the number of 'tenths' across.

When it comes to working out the number of tenths of a point within a grid square, as in step two above, estimation by eye is usually good enough. However, for accuracy, a romer can be used. This is a rectangular scale printed on the base plate of some of the more expensive models of compass or on special measuring cards. Or you can make your own from a piece of card. Each scale of map needs its own romer. The measuring scale printed on the last page of the book can also be pressed into service.

Chapter 2   SHAPE OF THE LANDSCAPE

"The soft curves of hills near Wenlock Edge in Shropshire."

The beauty of the countryside stems more from its shape or **relief** than from anything else. From the stark craggy mountains of the Scottish highlands to the subtle folds of the chalk downs in southern England, we delight in the interplay of hill, slope and valley. Relief is defined precisely on our maps, allowing the skilled map reader to form a picture of any landscape in the comfort of an armchair at home and, on the walk, to describe the route ahead.

To depict landscape, the map maker uses a special tool, **contours**. These, together with **spot heights** and rock markings, let you pick out the relief from the map and find the best walks; those with good views, the desired steepness of ascent, protection from the wind, or whatever the needs of the day may be. What's more, precise calculations can be made to help plan the walk. How long will it take to do the morning climbs? Is that slope too steep to descend safely?

Once under way, contour interpretation is the most powerful of navigational tools, particularly when paths, buildings, woods, and other symbols are lacking. By reading the contours we can say for example, 'the next path turns off just after we have reached the bottom of the valley' or 'ascend this slope diagonally until we reach a rocky knoll'. Contours provide some of the best clues for finding the way.

A word of encouragement is needed. When just starting to look seriously at contours, many people have difficulty in interpreting them well enough to form a mind-picture of the shape of the land. If you are finding that you cannot separate the ups from the downs, don't be discouraged and do persevere. Work at it when out walking and spend time at home making comparisons between the many map extracts and photographs scattered through the book. You will get there in the end, and the rewards are profound.

Contours, spot heights and rock features

Contours are imaginary lines on the map that join points of equal height above sea level. The vertical height between the contour lines is the **vertical interval** and this will always be defined in the key of

Parkhouse Hill

Landranger 119

The dramatic shapes of Chrome and Parkhouse hills in the Peak District are etched by the contour patterns in the map. Careful study is needed to work out the height of Chrome Hill.

The 400m contour height left of Chrome Hill is a clue. An index contour exists on Chrome Hill too, which must also be 400m; so the two thin contours inside that index contour make the hill's height 420m.

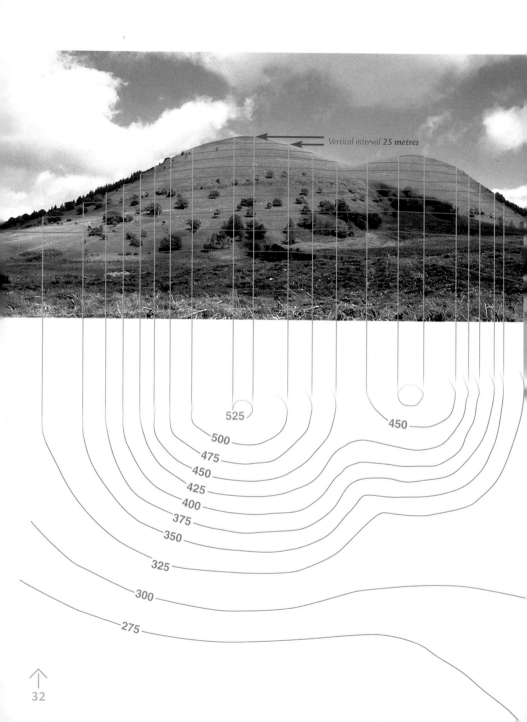

Vertical interval **25 metres**

525

450

500

475

450

425

400

375

350

325

300

275

Landranger 20
Intermediate contours are missing
on steep slopes. Contour heights
printed upside down indicate a slope
rising to the south.

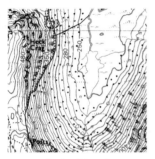

Outdoor Leisure 5
The contour vertical interval is
10m. on this map.

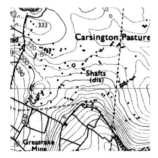

Outdoor Leisure 24
The contour vertical interval is
5m. on this map.

the map you are using. To illustrate the principle, see the photograph and diagram on page 32. Contour interpretation has two aspects: the spacing of the contours indicating steepness and the curves they make as they follow hillsides around indicating the shape of the land, known as **relief**.

Besides contours, spot heights (e.g. '760' in the extract left) record their height in metres above sea level, as do all trig. points. We shall see shortly how they help us to interpret relief.

Maps also record the presence of rock, where it outcrops through the vegetation cover. Where this occurs, chiefly in the wilder parts of the country, the markings help to show relief by highlighting the steeper slopes, although some rock markings show level outcrops. Look at the map keys for a definition of the different sorts of outcrop.

To summarise the rules for contours on Landranger and Explorer maps:
- Contours and spot heights show heights in metres above sea level.
- The vertical interval on Landranger is 10m. On Explorer it is 5m in lowland areas but 10m in upland areas; you need to check the key of the map you are using. (As a guide, 10m is roughly the height of the roof ridge of a normal two storey house).
- Every fifth contour (**index contour**) is printed more thickly, to help with counting between contours and following lines around hills.
- Where space permits, contour lines are numbered with their height, always printed so that the top of the number points uphill.
- On Landranger only, if the slope is too steep for the four intermediate thinner contour lines to be drawn separately, some or all of them are missed out. The thick contours are always present. As a rule of thumb, when just one of the thin contour lines is missing, the slope steepness is about 1 in 3.
- Contours continue under rock features, the black markings being simply overprinted.

Examples of Contour Relief

In the rich variety of Britain's landscape, nature has produced many different scenes, varying from the flat meadows of the Fens to the complex cwms and cliffs of Snowdonia. No matter how complicated the relief may be, it is in fact made up of a number of basic shapes which repay a little study.

Have a look at the pairs of map extract and photograph on these pages, taken mainly from the Lake District (one from the Peak District), which illustrate these landforms and their representation by contours. Examine each photo carefully and compare it with the contours in the extract that lie in the area of view. The contours have been copied from Outdoor Leisure maps to strip out all irrelevant detail.

Concentric rings depict an isolated HILL, even if as in this case the rough ground makes the contours irregular. The contours are spaced more closely on the left, where the slope is steeper.

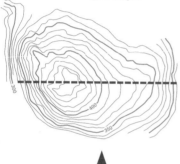

Binsey, in the north west of the Lake District

A SADDLE is the intersection of the route between two valleys that ascends least and and the link between two hills that descends least.

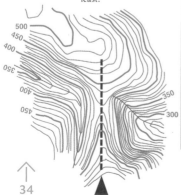

Looking from Scales Fell to Souther Fell, in the Lake District

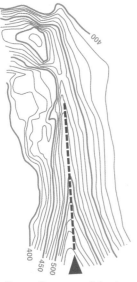

Contour lines are parallel and none cross the RIDGE in its level part in the middle.

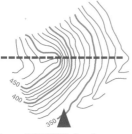

Since a CONCAVE slope is steeper near the top, its contour lines are spaced more closely there.

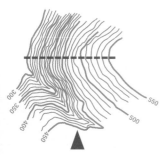

Since a CONVEX slope is steeper near the bottom, its contour lines are spaced more closely there. A danger when descending is not being able to see what is to come.

Rushup Edge, Mam Tor behind, in the Peak District

White Hause silhouetted against Dead Crags, Skiddaw behind

Western slopes of Watson's Dodd in the Lake District

Techniques for contour interpretation

There are a number of techniques to help with recognising relief from contours, some fairly fundamental whilst others are better classified as useful tricks.

Getting a feel for the relief of an area

The first aim of any mapreader on opening the map of an unfamiliar piece of countryside is to try to visualise the terrain, which means first and foremost getting a handle on the shape of the land.

Referring to the map on the opposite page of the Shropshire landscape by Wenlock Edge, try the following:

Returning to the map from page 31, how high is Parkhouse Hill? Bottom left of the extract is the index contour line 400m. If you count down two index lines from there, Dowall Hall is seen to be on the 300m line. Follow this round to the foot of Parkhouse Hill. Now go up one index line (350m) and one thin line to the top of the hill, which must be on or just above 360m.

Landranger 119

- *Scan the area and note the main parts where contour lines are packed close together – these are the major slopes.*

A wood lies from **A** to **A**. Through this a steep slope descends NW to Byne Brook. To the SE of this slope, there are three shorter steep slopes **B**.

- *Look at the spot heights and numbers on contour lines and identify parts that are generally high or generally low.*

These should relate to the slopes already identified. The long crest line of the first slope has heights of 240, 209 and 220, whilst the hills above the steeper slopes are at 320, 300 and 323, the highest on the map. The lowest parts lie to the NW of the edge by Byne Brook (138 and 150) and to the SE of the map (153 and 138).

- *Scan for the crest line of the main ranges of hills, as indicated by the tell-tale enclosed contour rings of hill tops.*

The crest line above the slope **A** to **A** has elongated rings all at 240m, and there are ring contours above each of the slopes **B** (330m, 310m and 320m).

- *Look for major rivers and streams, their valleys should be dominant features.* The streams **C** have cut deep valleys.

- *Identify areas with few contour lines, either lowland (usually) or upland plains.* Look at the NW and SE corners of the extract.

Landranger 137

Once you have worked out the general relief pattern in this way, you have a framework on which to hang the detail of a part that you are particularly interested in.

Recognising hill and mountain tops

These always consist of a closed rings of contours. They may not be well formed circles, indeed they could be highly irregular, but if they form a complete ring, they indicate a top.

Calculating the height of a point

The first step is to fix the contour line on which the point lies – or the nearest line on either side. The question then is, "what is the height of this 'target' contour line?" Scan the map for the nearest number on a contour line, or use a spot height to give a value to an adjacent contour line. Then follow this known contour line along its length until it nears the target line. Count lines up or down from the known line to calculate the height of the target line. When counting lines of a large height difference, just count the intervening thick lines, multiply by five and then add the extra thin lines at either end. Height difference is the number of lines multiplied by the contour interval.

Calculating height difference

You will often need to do this when working out the length of time to allow for hills when planning a walk (Chapter 7). Either work out the height of the lower and higher points and take the difference, or count the contour lines between the two and multiply by the contour interval.

Reading slope direction

The slope rises and falls at right angles to the contour lines, but it may not be obvious which direction is 'up' and which is 'down'. If a nearby

A chalk valley in the Chilterns. Can you relate the snaking line of the valley before you in the photo to the curving "Vs" of the contours highlighted in pink on the map?

In the map, the way the contour line numbers are printed indicates land rising to the north. Thus "Vs" pointing to the north are valleys, to the south spurs. See diagram on page 40.

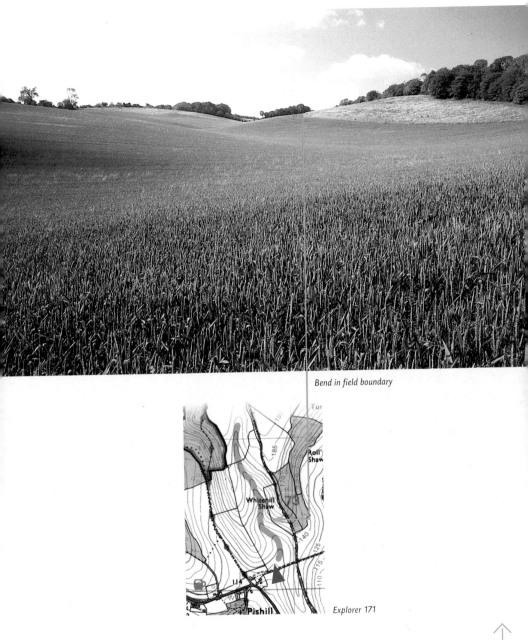

Bend in field boundary

Explorer 171

stream does not make the slope direction clear, it can be revealed by spot heights or numbered contour lines bracketing the point.

Alternatively, as contour line heights are always printed with the top of the figures pointing uphill, look for the nearest figure, and follow its contour line round to as near your point as possible, remembering which is 'up' as your eye follows the line.

A valley or a spur?

Sometimes the contours zigzag across the map in a succession of wiggles and it is not always obvious which are valleys and which are spurs. Often the valleys are clearly indicated by the presence of streams.

Where this is not the case, such as in chalk or limestone areas, we can use the fact that the contours of both valleys and spurs are shaped into a series of 'Vs', (or maybe more like 'Us'). The 'Vs' all conform to the following rule:

- If the 'Vs' point uphill, it is a valley.
- If the 'Vs' point downhill, it is a spur.

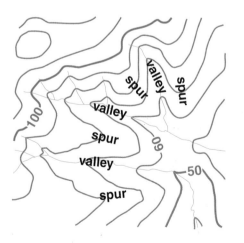

"Easy walking in North Yorkshire."

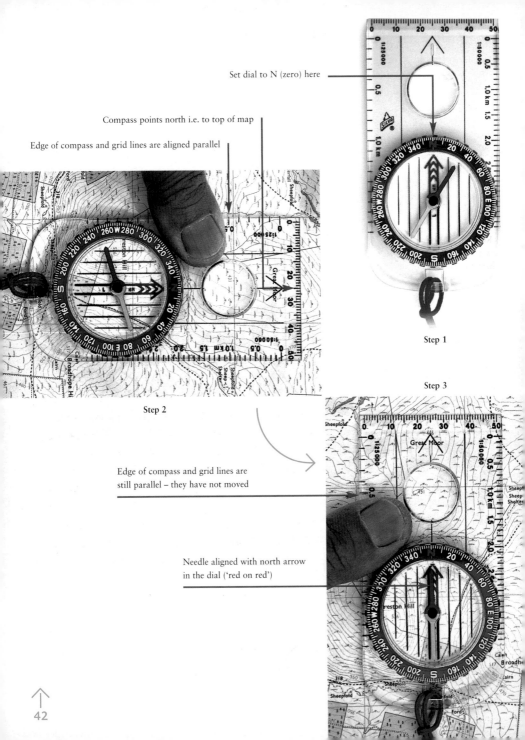

Set dial to N (zero) here

Compass points north i.e. to top of map

Edge of compass and grid lines are aligned parallel

Step 1

Step 2

Step 3

Edge of compass and grid lines are still parallel – they have not moved

Needle aligned with north arrow in the dial ('red on red')

Setting the Map by Compass

Step 1

Set the N on the dial to the arrow line on the base.

Step 2

Place the compass near the edge of the map with its edge parallel to a north pointing grid line (with the compass pointing to north on the map).

Step 3

Keeping a firm grip on the compass, turn the whole map and compass round until the compass needle is aligned with the arrow in the dial. The map is now set.

Having seen what a map is and its varied devices for depicting the countryside, it is now time to learn some of the basic skills needed to navigate a walk. This is best done with an understanding of how a walk is navigated.

Before setting out, you will have worked out your route on the map. Once on the walk, the act of navigating this route is not a continuous process, as you do not want to go along with your face constantly buried in the map. Rather, as we shall see, you divide the route up into many often quite short legs, and navigate each of these as a separate exercise. For each leg you do the following:

- *Pinpoint current location – this chapter*.
- *Choose the route for the leg – next chapter*.
- *Follow the instructions for the leg, enjoying the walk – following chapter*.

Setting the map

For pinpointing your current location, and for many other map reading actions, you will be constantly relating map to ground and ground to map, the bread and butter of navigation. This process is always helped by first **setting the map**. That is to say: rotating the map until the features on the map line up with their counterparts on the ground, just as the map extracts in this book mirror the direction of the photos alongside.

With the map set, the symbol of a church for instance on the map lies in the same direction from your position as the real church is in the country. Likewise a hill over there to the right will be seen over on the right of the map.

And when you have set the map, you will find the north edge of the map will also be pointing to north on the ground.

You can set the map four ways; setting the map by compass (left), setting the map by compass – a simple way, setting the map by clip-on compass, or finally a visual link by features.

**Warning
when setting the map.**

Remove the map case cord from around your neck. If you don't, either you can't turn the map round properly or you will strangle yourself!

Just hold the map case in your hand as you walk unless you are on a long obvious leg with little navigating to do.

Purchase a Silva Type 19
Clip-on Compass, and clip it onto
your map inside the map case
before starting the walk.

Also insert a Clippy Card under the
compass, aligning the card carefully
with the grid lines on the map, as
described on the card. On the walk,
to set the map all you have to do is
rotate the map as described in the
photograph below.

The beauty of this is you can set
the map at any time with the
minimum of fuss. Also, as you are
not distracted by having to hold a
compass on the map, you can
concentrate on the map reading,
using one hand to hold the map
and the index finger of the other to
point to your position.

Setting the map by compass – a simple way

*Just drop your baseplate compass into your map case. Whenever you
need to set the map, turn the map until the compass needle points to
north on the map, ignoring the rest of the compass. This method may
not be as accurate as others but will do for simple tasks like checking
path direction.*

Setting the map by clip-on compass

*The photo shows the clip-on compass backed by a special card with
prominent red and white lines (see page 127). This is a card I have
designed – the **Clippy Card** – that does two things. Most importantly
it provides easily visible lines against which to align the compass needle
(much simpler to use than the sometimes difficult-to-see grid lines),
and it lets you allow for magnetic variation.*

*Owners of this book can easily make up their own cards by turning
to last page of the book. Here are two samples to cut out and mount
on card or, even better, to take to an office supplies shop to have the
card encapsulated in plastic.*

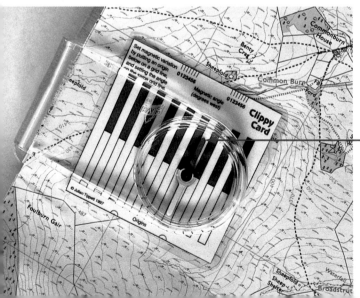

Turn the map round until the needle
lies parallel with the red and white
lines on the Clippy Card (*red on red*).

Setting the map by features

Although this map of Turville 'reads' the right way it does not match the features on the ground. So the map has to be rotated as below to align to the features.

The correct setting of the map to features. In this case the footpath on the map lines up with the same footpath on the ground.

The advantage of setting the map by compass

Setting the map by compass has the advantage over setting by features that you don't need to pinpoint your position to do it. This can come in handy when you are not quite sure of where you are and want to start identifying features about you to locate your position on the map.

Setting the map by features

Imagine you are standing on the hill above Turville as in the photo. To set the map here you would put your finger on your present location (the red arrow in the map extract), and then turn the map round until the village of Turville on the map lies directly ahead of you, just as the map extract below is aligned.

To be accurate you would have to identify a particular point in the village, such as the church, and line that up on both map and ground. Instead of an object in the distance like the church, you can use a linear feature, such as the footpath down to Turville.

Setting the map by features is generally less useful than by compass, as it works only when prominent landmarks exist to set the map by, the set map then being used to identify more subtle features.

Using a set map

Once you have set the map (and keep it set – don't let it drift into a different direction!), you can interpret the landscape from the map and vice versa. The map seems to come alive. When it is set:

- *a line from your position through an object on the map will point to the same object on the ground*
- *and vice versa, a line from an object on the ground to your position will go through the object on the map*
- *if an object lies to the left (or right) of another object visible on the*

Chapel

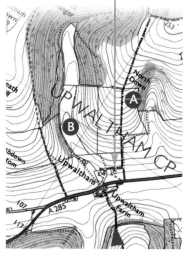

Explorer 121

Handy Tip

When projecting lines from your position on the set map to objects on the ground, you will find it helpful to hold a straight edge on the map. You could use the edge of the measuring ruler provided in the last page of this book.

Beware using the edge of a second compass as its magnetic needle might affect the needle of the clip-on compass.

We think we are at the red arrow on the map. What clues in both map and photo confirm this?

We are on a left hand bend in the track leading down to a farm on a main road.

The detail of the buildings etc. beyond the road match well, although the field boundary beyond the small church is missing on the ground.

The spur and valley sequence coming towards us down to the main road is accurately reflected in the pattern of 'Vs' on the map (pointing uphill in the valleys and downhill on the spurs).

Note how the tracks at points **A** and **B** are pointing directly to us, both on ground and the map.

ground, then it will lie similarly to the left (or right) on the map.

● your route ahead lies in the same direction on map and ground. In fact you can use the route on the map as a pointer for your way on the ground, making other ways of using the compass for this purpose unnecessary.

Pinpoint your position

We have seen that a walk is done as a series of informally chosen legs, and the first act before starting the leg is to pinpoint position. (If you cannot do this you are lost!) On most occasions, you will have a pretty good idea of where you are because you have kept track of progress mentally since the last fix, but every so often you will become more uncertain and need to confirm your position securely.

How do you do this? First, set the map and identify your supposed position. Then select some features you can see about you that should be recorded on the map; you simply confirm that the map and ground positions of each object are on a line radiating from your current position.

The features you choose will depend a lot on what you can see. It should be relatively easy with objects such as a church with spire, the path you are walking along, or a distinctive hill; you might even be in the happy state (from a position finding point of view only!) of standing on a bridleway under an electricity transmission line – unmistakable! In practice the lining up is done informally, not treated as a mathematical exercise, and should quickly become a subconscious act.

But what if one or more features do not fit? You will then have to question whether you might not be at your pinpointed map position or whether you have pinpointed position correctly but one of the features has changed since the map was printed.

In this latter case, enough other features should fit to satisfy you that the fault lies with the map, not yourself. In more difficult country, possibly in forest or in mist, unmistakable features might be lacking.

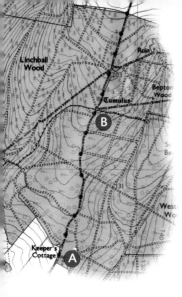

Explorer 120

Observation from the map

Our route goes up the curved bridleway north from Keeper's Cottage **A** and turns right at junction **B**. How will we recognise the turning when we get to it, allowing that it might not be waymarked?

Rather than engage in the trying task of judging distance to it by timing how long it will take to get there, we can spot enough unique features of the junction to be able to recognise it securely when we reach it:

It's just across a fence or other boundary (incidentally also a parish boundary)

The forest track the bridleway follows turns off only half right, the first turning having this angle. It descends gradually.

There is also a track off half left, ascending gently.

No other junction on the way up has this unique combination of properties.

You will then have to use ingenuity, perhaps by checking path directions or interpreting local relief by contours.

Observation

To get the most out of map reading keen eyes and an alert mind are essential. Good observation is important both in extracting detail from the map and in looking for clues in the countryside.

Thus you might spot a smaller path going off to the right of the forestry track you are walking along. Maybe that is your next path, rather than the more obvious forest track. Or, you are looking for the point where your next path leaves a straight and featureless bridleway. You see a dip in the path that shows up in the map contours, telling you how far along the bridleway you have progressed. When walking across a patchwork of fields you will always keep an eagle eye open for the next stile on the far side of each field.

"Keep an eagle eye open for the next stile."

"Slaters Bridge, Little Langdale in the Lake District. Footbridges are marked as FB on 1:25,000 maps."

Pant-glas

Landranger 148

Bends in the path

Often the very best features to navigate by are staring you in the face, namely the bends in the path or track you are walking along. They show up clearly on the map and, because of foreshortening, even more so on the ground as seen here by comparing map and photo.

Can you identify on the map right hand and left hand bends met on the way down to Pant-glas?

In mist or in a forest it helps to know that on a long sweeping bend you can even judge exactly how far round it you have walked by using the set map or a compass. Your position is at the point where the path direction on the map agrees with your current direction on the ground.

Handy Tip 1

When reading a route always keep the map turned round so that the route is going away from you.
Then you won't get mixed up between the 'lefts' and the 'rights'.

Handy Tip 2

Read enough from the map to be able to follow the path without having to rely on the path being well waymarked.

In practice the route finding will usually turn out to be easy as, in addition to the features you read from the map, you will have footpath signposts, arrows and stiles to show the way, not to mention a trodden path across the fields. But in less frequented places you will have to rely solely on mapped features to point the way.

Since a map is a kind of picture of the landscape, it comes as no surprise that you can make mental images from it of what will be seen on the ground as you walk along. This ability helps at two stages: planning your walk, see Chapter 7, and when navigating on the walk itself, the subject of this chapter.

What matters is the·role the map plays in providing images to use for directions to point the way. You will use the map to formulate a set of instructions for finding the way, in effect turning the map into your own personalised guidebook. This is the **Choose the route** *step in walking a leg of your walk.*

See the extract and directions in the margin of page 52. What can be said about these instructions? They are as clear as those taken from an average guide book, and are given in a way that is practicable to follow. The instructions say 'right' or 'left', much more useful as walking directions than 'north' or 'south'. Using Explorer maps, you could devise such instructions for any itinerary of footpaths anywhere in the country.

With Landranger maps, references to field boundaries could not be made and distance measurement would be less precise. Nevertheless, the instructions would still be good enough, provided that you could be sure of seeing the footpaths clearly marked on the ground with waymarks, stiles or a beaten track. Much more could have been included, perhaps the views and more on the slopes. But there is enough there for accurate navigation.

The secret is to choose from the available features those most useful for describing the route. If field boundaries and buildings are not present, you will have to use contours to describe the relief in a way that is helpful to route finding.

No two routes are the same and often ingenuity is needed. You will see that instructions of this sort are essential to the process of route finding, so it pays to grasp every opportunity of practising the art of formulating them. Do it at home, sitting in your favourite armchair. One of my most pleasant forms of escapism is to pore over the map of an attractive walking area, and to work out a number of

Explorer 152

Our next leg takes us from the pond at Home Farm to the gap between the two woods by point **A**.

In practice it might be better to split this into two shorter legs, but here we take the full leg. How can it be put into words?

"Take the unfenced track to the right of the pond. Ascend gently for 500m round a right hand bend to the end of the track, in a valley going down to the left.

Now turn left to go by footpath over fields. Cross three fields with a bend to the right on entering the second field. The last field is crossed on a gently rising course.

The path heads for the gap between the woods at the top of the third field."

Much more could be said, but this is enough to define the route (and enough to remember). If walking the leg does not go smoothly, we can go later into such detail as that the boundary between fields two and three is itself in a small valley.

walks to follow on an eagerly awaited visit there, and I'll sometimes do this even if I have no plans to go there.

Attention to detail

Students often exclaim at the amount of detail the map maker manages to cram in. Not only is there such a lot in each map, objects are placed with great precision. Take advantage of this by reading the map closely. Note for example where a path does not cross a road directly; rather it starts again on the other side a few metres to the left. Such care will help when looking for that footpath on your walk. Read not just the basic minimum of information from the map, but take out more details than you strictly need, so as to be able to cope when some features cannot be seen on the ground or the map contains a mistake.

Map memory

The suggestion that the route from Home Farm (left) should be split into two parts springs from the thought that the route description is too long to hold in memory whilst walking the leg. You would forget some of the details long before reaching the two woods. But there is much to gain from cultivating this type of memory, as the better it is the longer the legs you can choose, and the longer you can enjoy your walk before having to stop and check the map again. It is this ability which lets you do a walk without having constantly to consult the map.

Getting from A to B

Most walk legs can be described simply using obvious features such as field boundaries, tracks and paths marked on the ground.

Sometimes such features may be lacking or it is not obvious how to use them. Then you need to devise a strategy for describing the leg and then walking it. On the following pages are a few ideas for the routes, marked in yellow going upwards on the map.

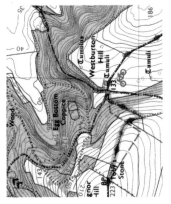

Explorer 121

RIGHTS OF WAY NOT PRESENT ON THE GROUND

Arriving at Toby's Stone, it is highly
likely the green bridleways will not
be visible on the ground,
as there are no black path or track
markings on their line.
Expect to follow the track ahead,
bend right and then turn sharp left
onto another track.

Outdoor Leisure 21

BUILDING AS CHECK POINT

The two small buildings at
Flower Scar will provide a useful
check as the track bends sharp
right before ending at a wall.
From here our route goes left
across the angle of a field to its
far lower corner.
From there the path follows a
wall with the stream valley falling
away to the left. It is uncertain on
which side of the wall the path
goes, probably on the left
of the wall.

Outdoor Leisure 6

UNFENCED ROAD

We need to pick up the track that
descends to the left of the wood
ahead. It branches off the track we
are following on entering an area
of rough ground, where the tracks
become unfenced.

COUNT THE BRIDGES

The problem is
how do we recognise the path
turning off to the left at point **B**
after walking three kilometres up
the white road (a former railway)
in the valley bottom.
All the way woods will line the
sides as we walk alongside the river
and nothing obvious marks the
turning. And this state of affairs
persists beyond. Keeping track of
the gaps in the woods could be
done but would take a lot of
attention. The path turns left by
the first building(s) met near the
track, but might these be hidden
behind trees?

The answer in this case is to keep
track of where you are by counting
the bridges you cross and noting
which side of the river you are on.
At **B** you have just crossed the
tenth bridge and are on the right
hand side of the river having passed
a gap in the woods on the left.

Landranger 119

A PHYSICAL FEATURE

We have been ascending the path to point **A** where it is going up a spur. There is no path from here to point **B**.

The contours show we can follow the rim of a scooped valley, the directions from **A** being **Keep left, following the top rim of the steep slope down to the left.** The rim ascends gently curving left, then levels out. From the point where the rim of the steep slope left starts to descend (approx point **C**), we can take a compass bearing to point **B**.

Outdoor Leisure 21

SLOPE DIRECTION

There is no trampled path on the ground to follow. From the stream crossing go straight up the fall line of the slope until the ground levels off. Bear right to go parallel with the slope up on your left, until you see your gentle descent to the left end of the wood.

Outdoor Leisure 16

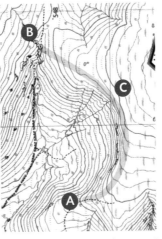

Outdoor Leisure 4

ALLOW FOR ERROR

From its junction with the bridleway at **A**, our path starts ascending, following a small stream to our right. After about 300m we should fork left on a path that goes left of the brow of the hill ahead.

Perhaps in mist, suppose we miss this fork? When we reach the crest of the ridge, if the path ahead bears right and starts to descend, and we cannot then see a wood 100m to our left, then we know we must have missed the fork earlier and now must go left along the ridge to pick up the correct path.

"Stepping stones, here across the West Dart river in Dartmoor, are written in full on 1:25,000 maps."

Building up your own map reading tool kit

You will probably start your route-finding career by getting to know the map symbols and using these to navigate by. These will serve you well in easy country but later you will come across terrain that requires more sophisticated techniques. As soon as possible you will add contour interpretation to your repertoire, along with the compass, distance measurement and estimation, some hill techniques, and a host of smaller 'tricks of the trade'. You should aim to build a toolkit such that, no matter the problem, you can always find an answer, often using techniques in combination with each other. With time you will develop your own personal style of map reading.

Quite often there are a number of different ways to solve a problem. None need be better or worse than the other, the only valid test being 'does it work for you?'

"Descending Higger Tor to cross moorland to Stanage Edge in the Peak District."

Navigation Drill

1. *Pinpoint your position on the map.*

2. *Select the next leg on the route and memorise instructions for it.*

3. *Set off in the correct direction.*

4. *Follow the instructions, enjoying the walk.*

We have seen that the best way to progress along a route is by means of a series of usually quite short legs, each leg adopting the drill of **pinpointing position, choosing the route for the next leg,** and then **walking the leg**. The reason for adopting such a process is to keep the map reading under control, since route finding for most people is a means to an end. They take a walk for the views, for the exercise, or whatever, but rarely just for the map reading. The navigation has to be efficient, but it should also be unobtrusive.

It is true that on rare occasions the navigation will get difficult or a mistake will be made and then, adrenalin flowing, route finding takes over the whole of the navigator's attention. Success in overcoming such problems can be counted as a real bonus. But for most of the time walkers want route finding to take place virtually unnoticed.

How does this navigation drill let you find the way securely, whilst leaving time to enjoy the walk? It does this by:

- Concentrating the map reading into short bursts for committing directions to memory.
- Using these memorised directions when actually walking, thereby leaving you free to concentrate on enjoying the ramble.

Before looking at how it works in practice, for completeness one further step needs to be added to the process. After having stopped to do the map reading before a leg you need to take particular care that, when you set off to continue the walk, you set off in the correct direction. It is easy to get disoriented when concentrating on the map. Navigation drill thus becomes the four steps as highlighted above left.

Navigation Drill - an example

We have reached the 'T' junction in the minor road by Hatchmans. From here we want to go past Bacres Farm and take the path that goes due west to the fork in the tracks in Barn Wood. The navigation of this next stretch might go as follows:

The start of the path to
Bacres Farm.

Arriving at the fork in the
tracks in Barn Wood.
Walkers here in the Chilterns will
recognise the white arrows of
the Chiltern Society who do the
waymarking. They use white
arrows in place of the usual yellow
for a footpath.

1. *Pinpoint Position.*

*We stand at the start of the path to Bacres Farm (red arrow) as seen
from the signpost of a footpath leaving a metalled road, and the path
going diagonally across the new crop, both visible in the photo. If we
turn round half right we would see the junction of minor roads. Map
and ground tally in all these respects.*

2. *Select next leg on route and memorise instructions for it.*

*We have chosen to go next to the fork in tracks in Barn Wood, the
yellow stripe defining the route there. If we were very tentative the leg*

Passing Bacres Farm. The sign reads "Beware ducks crossing".

The right hand bend 50m away is visible.

could be taken in two – to Bacres Farm and then to the fork – but this leg should be OK. **Directions:** *'Go diagonally across the field to Bacres Farm, there to pick up the track going straight ahead. After passing Bacres Farm on your right and a further 50m on, this track turns right; from there ascend inside the left-hand side of the wood for 500m to the fork.' Another person might come up with different words, which does not matter if they work all right.*

3. Set off in the correct direction.

No problem here – it's on the path across the field.

4. Follow the instructions.

Enjoy the walk. In this case the instructions will be easy to follow.

How long should a leg be?

The incentive to make a leg as long as possible, is the prospect of reducing the number of times needed to stop and consult the map. The less time spent map reading the more is left over for the views. Exceptionally, in the Lake District say, right at the start of the walk you might be able to see the full round of hills to be done. Only one leg for the whole day! But on the flip side of this coin, long legs make for

What if you forget the directions as you walk?

Or, equally common, the features you see on the leg are not as you had expected them to be. Either way you lose confidence in walking the leg.

No matter. Just stop immediately, look at the map, and begin a new leg from wherever you find yourself to be, starting of course with pinpointing your new position.

Forming a sense of distance

Here are some exercises to do on your walks. Do not use distances of more than a kilometre:

1. *Read map distances from where you are to places you can see, and assess the distances on the ground.*

2. *Do it the other way round: estimate distances to places you can see and then check your answers on the map.*

3. *Quote short distances to be walked during the next leg, say across a field, and assess what they 'feel' like.*

4. *After finishing a leg, before getting to grips with the next, estimate how far you have walked from a recent point, and check your answer on the map.*

Try to stick to one scale of map, say 1:25,000, and develop a feel for this.

much to remember. Thus, intricate map reading makes for short legs, and simple navigating for longer ones. And the better your map memory, the longer the legs you can cope with, something to develop with experience and practice.

A sense of distance

As an extra safeguard, it is a great help to carry in your memory not only your set of detailed directions but also a sense of how far you need to walk to reach the features you have chosen. In the Bacres Farm example (opposite page) the directions included two distance measurements of 50m and 500m; as you walk these stretches you would have a 'feel' for what 50m or 500m seems like on the ground.

Thus with such a sense, when you are walking to a target, alarm bells start ringing if you have covered the distance but the target has not yet come into sight. Suppose, having turned right after Bacre Farm, you do not recognise the fork in the tracks, walk past and are well on the way to Built Farm. Your sense of distance pulls you up short, long before you can get into serious trouble, and you can check what if anything is wrong. Without this sense you might carry blithely on for a long time, possibly getting heavily lost in the process. (In this example, you would also stop when the track unexpectedly leaves the wood and you see Built Farm half left, something you were not expecting.)

As you might expect, this knack comes mainly with experience. Even so, you can help it to grow by getting into the habit of quoting distances to yourself as you read the map. Say, 'We enter the wood in 150m' or 'The path junction comes 400m after the bridge', and so on. To be able to do this you need to measure short distances on the map. If you are using an OS 1:25,000 map and happen to be working near an edge, you could take advantage of the 100m divisions in the border. Or, if your eye is good enough, you could subdivide a grid square nearby into tenths and apply these to the distance to be measured. For more accurate work you should use the special measuring scale to cut out from the last page of this book.

Landranger 124

Most modern compasses have a millimetre scale and many, like the one used in illustrations in this book, have scales giving a direct read-out of hundreds of metres. You must choose the scale that tallies with your scale of map.

Let us measure from the bend in the track after Bacres Farm to the fork: on the map (below left) the correct measuring scale has been chosen for the map scale of 1:25,000. The fork lies 550m from the bend, however when using a millemetre rule on the same map (right)

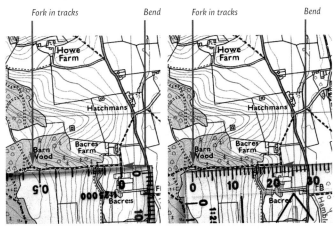

1:25,000 Scale Measure on Explorer 172   Millimetre Scale Measure on Explorer 172

a conversion to metres is needed. One millimetre at 1:25,000 scale = 25 metres and one millimetre at 1:50,000 scale = 50 metres. The distance between the fork and bend measures 22mm, multiplied by 25m = 550 metres.

A sense of distance has to do with informal estimating. In Chapter 7 the more rigorous job of measuring distance on the ground is covered.

A sense of direction

In the next chapter we shall see how the compass points the way accurately and helps in other ways. Besides using the compass,

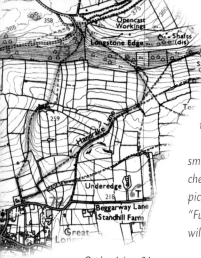

Outdoor Leisure 24

PRACTICE WALK 1

Length 3km. This route puts a premium on accurate route finding by field boundaries. There are a number of varied land shape features to keep you busy with the contours.

Explorer 182

PRACTICE WALK 2

With a length of 3km this walk would take only 40 minutes at a brisk pace, but you will take double this or more to explore all the detail on the map as you go.

a good navigator carries with him a 'sense' for direction, less precise but always there. You have in mind the 'big picture' surrounding your walk, which might be a range of hills, the sun or even the wind.

As you progress across the countryside by means of the small navigational decisions shown earlier in this chapter, you can check these, almost subconsciously, for consistency against the big picture to pick up errors early, before they have become serious. "Funny," you might say, "that hill shouldn't be over there." and so you will be prompted to check the map again.

There are three ways of doing this:

By features. You will try to fix your route in relation to a large hill or other feature that can be seen easily for much of the walk. For example, the photo and map extract on page 62 shows the view over a fairly complicated stretch of countryside in Southern Snowdonia.

If you are intending to take a route north east by public footpaths through the woods, when the views open up you would always expect to see the spine of high hills on your left hand side. Alarm bells ring if you see it ahead or on your right.

By the sun. Another time, you might be passing through some largish forests. You know that the general direction of the walk is south-west. Quite apart from any specific direction-finding by compass that you do, you would want to keep the sun (if you can see it that day) generally on your left in the morning, drifting round to straight ahead by mid-afternoon. Any significant deviation from this would give cause for concern.

By the wind. On high moors the wind direction can help in the same way. The weather forecast might have promised strong south-westerlies that day, which you can check out on the day against landmarks you can see. Later, when walking west in poor visibility, you would want to keep the wind on your left cheek. Going north east it would be blow from behind.

A word of warning, though. Wind direction can be fickle as it can

change by 90 degrees or more in the course of a day and
it eddies in valleys and around hills.

Getting started

Our voyage into the mysteries of map reading
has progressed far enough for you to start doing
some walks using only a map to guide you
(plus a compass for setting the map). Here are few
tips to help make those early forays successful.

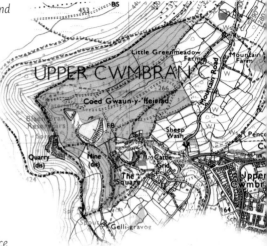

Explorer 152

Choice of route.

You will not need the full skills of planning a day's
walk (see Chapter 7) to settle upon these short practice
walks. Bear in mind:

- **Choose an area with a path network well marked on the ground.**
Best would be an area you are familiar with, but choosing a route
new to you within it. Ask an experienced walker for advice, or the staff
in a local outdoor shop, who will know good areas to try.
- *Make it short.* To allow time practising map reading, and to get
back in good time even if you make some mistakes.
- *Consider adapting a route from a guide book.* You could
transcribe its route to the map, leaving the book at home for the walk.

Marking your map.

One of the problems facing beginners is finding your place on
the map each time you stop to navigate. In early days, there appears to
be little pattern in all those lines on the map to guide your eye to
the place. Two tips:

- *Fold the map* to show the area of your walk, possibly detaching the
cover to do this more easily, and keeping the map in a map case.
- *Mark your route up* so that your eyes are immediately drawn to
the right part of the map. As you work your way round the route,
you will remember how far you have progressed. A highlighter pen

PRACTICE WALK 3

Length 5.5km. The start from the
car park looks quite complicated,
needing attention to detail to
find the way accurately. Once on
the way, route finding is easy and
there is much interesting map
reading to be done.

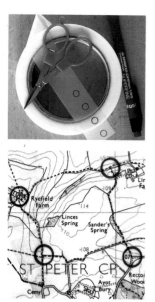

Make up your own reusable markers with 3Ms Removable Transparent Tape, on which circles are drawn with a fine permanent ink pen.

would be good, but it makes a permanent mark, however a much better solution is to make your own reuseable markers.

Out on the walk.

Devote some of these early walks to map reading practice and do the following:

- **Do navigation drill formally.** Later your own intuitive style can emerge which does not recognise the four distinct steps precisely.

- **Keep the map set when in use.** This takes a bit of practice as, when you start, you can set the map but find you are facing the wrong way, or the map is not between you and your route. Persevere.

- **Devote parts of the walk to specific topics.** Stop and compare the contours with the landscape. Recognise landmarks on map and ground. Do the distance estimating exercises on page 61. Look up unfamiliar symbols.

- **Take a spare map in the same series as your main map.** So you can refer to its table of symbols and other marginal information without having to to unfold the map you are using.

- **If you are learning with a companion.** Don't share, take a map and compass each.

I'm sure you will have great fun on these early map-only walks and get enormous satisfaction from completing them successfully. Good luck!

Chapter 6   THE COMPASS

"The descent from the summit of Sail to the saddle shown on page 16."

Outdoor Leisure 24

Here's a situation you meet when route-finding across fields.

You enter a large field with a hump in the middle, and there's no trampled path to point the way.

In this case there is a helpful signpost. If there were not, then a compass direction would help hit the field exit precisely.

Although experienced navigators look on the compass as an extraordinarily useful extra tool, they stress that it is strictly an extra. That is, the basis of navigation will always be good map reading, skill with the compass not being a substitute for this. When following a compass bearing, good navigators are constantly on the look-out for mapped features by which to fix position, perhaps a gully revealed by its contour shapes or a broken wall, the map being still very much in evidence. But enough of the caveats, what does a compass do for us?

The big new element brought by the compass is to show accurate direction on the ground – the direction of your next path or of a distant feature. Accurate direction comes into its own the moment mapped landmarks become too few and far between or are too confusing to work with. It becomes a treasured new clue. Even in lowland country with its wealth of features to navigate by, the compass is often invaluable. The three main compass techniques, accounting for 95% of its use, are to:

- Set the map – covered in Chapter 3.
- Point direction of the next path – covered this chapter.
- Plot a course over featureless land, often in mist – covered in Chapter 8, which also looks at some other compass techniques used in hill navigation.

Though a compass is basically a simple device, using it for the first time can be a curiously baffling experience. Fortunately, since it does not take long to make the breakthrough to confidence, it's worth getting to grips with the technique quickly so you can profit from it during your early map reading days when it will be particularly valuable.

Handy tip

Devote parts of your early practice walks to using the compass, and the set map. You need to check path direction by compass twenty times to learn the technique surely.

Magnetic poles, magnetic fields and maps

How does a compass work? It is a fact that the earth is a gigantic magnet with the magnetic poles located near (but not at) the geographical poles. Just like any magnet, the earth generates a magnetic field with lines of magnetic force connecting the two poles, and these lines of force are detectable at the earth's surface.

They are aligned generally in a north-south direction, though in certain localities such as Cape Town and the eastern and western coasts of North America, the angle between the magnetic line and the meridian of longitude (the **magnetic variation**) can reach as much as 30°. Fortunately for those of us who walk in Great Britain, magnetic variation nowhere exceeds 6°, is commonly 4°, and is diminishing year by year.

If a compass needle, itself a small magnet, is allowed to settle freely in the earth's magnetic field, it will line up with the local lines of magnetic force. Compass needles are usually painted so that the end pointing to north is coloured red. We shall look at magnetic variation later but since it is so small in the UK it can be safely ignored for the moment. In effect, we can say that the compass needle points to **north**.

Map north for us is that shown most conveniently on all OS maps, namely **grid north**, the direction of the north pointing grid lines. (The maps refer also to **geographical** or **true north**, which in the UK can be taken to be the same as grid north.)

Thus, in practical terms, the compass needle points to north on the ground, whilst the vertical grid lines point to north on the map. We now have solid references against which to plot the directions (or **bearings**) that we wish to walk.

Bearings and the protractor compass

A bearing is an angle that defines a direction i.e. the **direction of travel**. This might be the direction of a path, the route to be taken across a moor, or the direction of a distant hill we wish to locate. Bearings are defined by giving the number of degrees (between 0° and 360°) in a clockwise direction from north to the direction of travel (see Diagrams 1 and 2 which show the same bearing on ground and on map).

Diagram 1

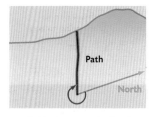

Path leads away at a bearing of approximately 300 degrees.

Diagram 2

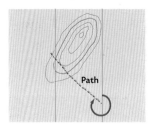

The same bearing as it would appear on the map.

A compass needle on its own cannot help in defining a bearing as it defines one direction only, i.e. north. Therefore a means is needed to set out the direction of travel in relation to the direction of north.

This is where the modern protractor (or **baseplate**) compass comes in, an elegant yet simple invention of Swedish orienteers. The essential parts of such a compass are as follows:

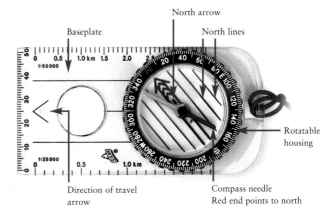

Diagram 3

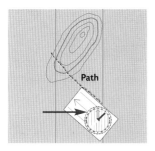

With the baseplate on the line of the path and housing rotated so northlines align with north pointing grid lines, the bearing 310 degrees can be read at the red arrow.
(Ignore compass needle when compass is on map).

Diagram 4

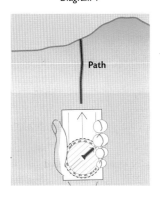

Check these parts with your own compass.
By placing it on the map, the compass can be set to the bearing of a path (Diagram 3). Its value in degrees can be read where the direction of travel line intersects the scale running around the housing (310° in this example).

Having set a map bearing on the compass, the compass can be taken off the map, held in the hand, and rotated until the compass needle and the orienting lines are aligned together. When this is done, the direction of travel arrow points along the direction of that bearing on the ground (Diagram 4). This is the direction in which to walk.

Now, having covered the basic principles, how can the compass be used in practice? The classical use of the compass, to plot a course in mist over featureless moorland, will be looked at in Chapter 8. Here we examine the less dramatic but no less useful technique of pointing along the direction of our next footpath, both using the compass as just outlined, but also by set map using the clip-on compass.

Point direction by compass

We have arrived at the junction at the tip of the red arrow on the map. The map and photo both show the path we have arrived on to the right with another path going left plus two others ahead. We wish to continue on the path highlighted in yellow on the map.
Which is it on the ground?
The compass will tell us.

Step A

Place the compass on the map with an edge of the base aligned to the desired path. Be sure the direction of travel arrow is pointing in the direction you want to walk the path, not in the reverse direction. Ignore the needle when the compass is on the map.

Step B

Holding the base firm, turn the housing round until the north lines on the compass are parallel with north-pointing grid lines. Be sure the north arrow is pointing to north on the map.

Our current location

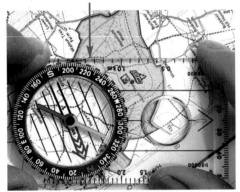

Step A

Our current location

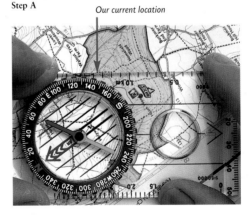

Step B

Step C
Take the compass
off the map and
hold it as above

Point path direction by compass

Even in quite straightforward country, it's amazing how often doubts
creep in about which path to take at a junction or, as you are walking
a path, whether you have chosen the right one. One answer to these
quandaries is to call on your compass for a second opinion.

Such doubts arise particularly in woods, which have a nasty habit of
supplying more or fewer paths than the number marked on the
map, with possibly disastrous results for the unwary map reader if the
main paths have not been well waymarked.

The compass confirms the choice of the path you want by pointing
accurately along its line. This works on the assumption that no two
paths in the vicinity lie in the same direction, a highly unlikely
occurrence.

Let us now assume we are following a walk from Arbon through
the beech woods of the Chilterns, and have come to the junction
marked with the red arrow in the map extract. We wish to continue
heading up the map on the yellow route. The map shows four
paths leaving this junction and we wish to be sure to take the correct
one. Follow steps A to D , which demonstrate in practice steps 3
and 4 in the diagrams on the previous page.

Step D
Keeping the compass pointing
away from you, turn your whole
body round until the needle
lines up with the north arrow
(red on red).

The direction of travel arrow
now points along the line of the
path you should take.

Point direction by set map

Step 1

Point on the map to your current location, and then turn the map round so that the path you want to follow is pointing directly away from you. The map should end up positioned as in the photo, ignoring the compass at this stage.

Step 2

Holding the map in this position, turn your whole body round until the compass needle is aligned with the Clippy Card lines (red on red), i.e. the map is set.

Then your path on the map points to the same path on the ground, as in the two photos.

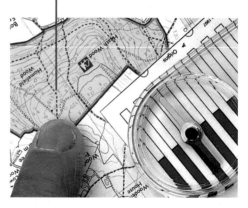

Point path direction by set map

Although using the path on the map to point the way is not so accurate as using the direction of travel arrow on a compass, because a short length of path is a less clear pointer, it is quite good enough for confirming the direction of a path. The set map method requires one step fewer than the traditional compass method and, since the clip-on compass is always 'at the ready' on your map, you will find this method quicker and easier to use.

Some warnings

Compasses of the type illustrated in this book, the standard walkers'
compass, can achieve an accuracy of plus or minus 4°, if care is taken.
This means in practice after 500m of walking on a bearing, you could
be up to 35m left or right of the correct point, a very acceptable level
of precision. However, on a rain-lashed mountain top, working
with cold gloved fingers, the compass sliding all over the wet plastic
map case, such accuracy is something of a pipe dream. Here are a few
relevant practical thoughts:

- *Get a companion to hold the map firm and horizontal.*
- *Take your gloves off, if you dare.*
- *After placing the compass base and turning the housing, recheck*
that the edge of the base and the orienting lines are still properly
aligned, and have not slipped.
- *Be sure you can see properly (e.g. take reading glasses, if needed).*
Take extra care in bad weather when rain drops and condensation can
obscure the map.
- *To guard against false readings, make certain that there are*
no steel objects or electro-magnetic fields nearby (fences ,electricity
cables, cars, etc.). Check whether any of your own belongings (watch,
camera, ice axe, lead pencil, etc.) could cause the needle to move on
being brought near to the compass and, if so, keep them well clear.

Beware the Three Big Compass Mistakes

Or you will find yourself pointing 180° in the wrong direction!
Mistake 1 *- do not put your compass on the map (step A) with the*
direction of travel arrow pointing back to your present position.
Mistake 2 *- do not rotate the housing (step B) so that the north lines*
point south on the map - or east or west.
Mistake 3 *- do not rotate your body (step C) so that the white end of*
*the needle is aligned with the north arrow. Remember it's **red on red**.*

Magnetic variation

When, in Step B (page 72) you align the north lines with the grid lines on the map, you set the grid bearing of the leg to be walked, i.e. the bearing is referenced to **grid north**. However, in Step D (page 73) the north arrow is aligned with the compass needle which points to **magnetic north** - you need a magnetic bearing set on the compass.

The difference between grid and magnetic north is the **magnetic variation**, defined on OS maps as **grid magnetic angle**, a small angle that currently (year 2000) varies from about 2° at Land's End to some 5° on the east coast, always west of north in this country. An 'average' magnetic variation of about 4° follows a line from the Isle of Wight, through the Lake District up to the Isle of Skye. If magnetic variation is 4° west, to ignore it will introduce an error of some 7% of distance travelled, pushing you to the left of the true course.

What's more, the magnetic poles are wandering slowly in position, with the result that magnetic variation is currently lessening by about one degree in 6 years. You therefore need to work out the value for any particular map and year; this can be calculated from information printed in the map margin, as seen here.

Approaching the mouth of the Mawddach estuary in Snowdonia with Barmouth lying beyond.

The Three Norths

Magnetic variation or grid magnetic angle. True North can be totally ignored by the walking fraternity.

NORTH POINTS

At the centre of this sheet true north is 1°04' west of grid north. Magnetic north is estimated at 4°21' west of grid north for Jul 2000. Annual change is approximately 11' east.

Explorer

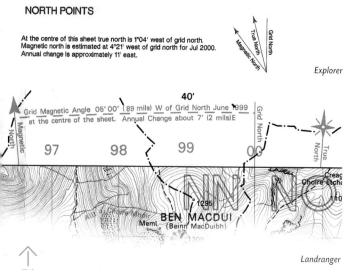

Grid Magnetic Angle 05° 00' (89 mils) W of Grid North June 1999 at the centre of the sheet. Annual Change about 7' (2 mils) E

97 98 99 00

BEN MACDUI
Meml (Beinn MacDuibh)

Landranger

Magnetic Variation

Magnetic variation can be calculated from the information supplied on the map. On Explorer maps look in the key. On Landranger maps look in the top margin.

76

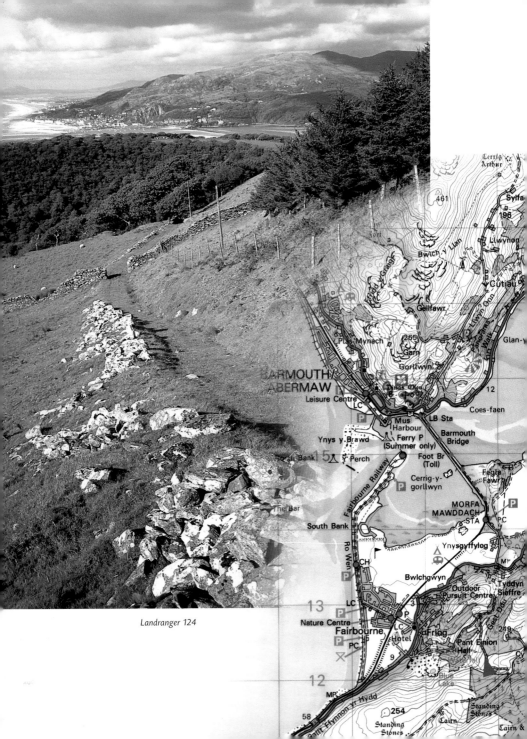

Landranger 124

Need we bother with magnetic variation?

Since magnetic variation is so small, it can be safely ignored when checking path direction, and when setting the map. You will not notice the error caused by disregarding it.

As for using the compass to plot a course over open country (see chapter 8), if magnetic variation exceeds 4°, it is worth allowing for as described in the text, though disregarding it here too will not have serious consequences.

Having worked out magnetic variation for your map, you can choose one of two ways to apply it (for the following examples we will assume it to be 4° west).

Method 1 (the usual method).

Having taken the grid bearing from the map (step B above), convert it to a magnetic bearing by adding the variation – 'Grid to Mag >Add'. In the photograph on page 101 the grid bearing taken from the map after step B is 101°; add 4° to make the magnetic bearing 105°. (In the example on page 72 magnetic variation was not applied.)

(Note: when working from ground to map – as in Chapter 8 page 103 onward – subtract magnetic variation to convert a magnetic bearing to a grid bearing – 'Mag to Grid >Get Rid')

Method 2.

A semi-permanent modification to your compass saves having to make this adjustment each time. Using a permanent (spirit-based) fine marker pen, draw a line on the compass housing (here a dark blue line has been drawn) from the 356° mark across the centre to the 176° mark i.e. assuming a magnetic variation of 4° west. Thereafter, when aligning the magnetic needle (i.e. using the compass off the map, step D), use this new line instead of the north arrow. Magnetic variation is then automatically allowed for. (The line can be removed safely with methylated spirits).

Chapter 7 PLANNING A WALK

"Woodland walk near Tarn Howes Cumbria." Photo Gordon Gadsby

The Country Code

Enjoy the countryside and respect its life and work.

Guard against all risk of fire.

Fasten all gates.

Keep your dogs under close control.

Keep to public paths across farmland.

Use gates and stiles to cross fences, hedges and walls.

Leave livestock, crops and machinery alone.

Take your litter home.

Help to keep all water clean.

Protect wild life, plants and trees.

Take special care on country roads.

Make no unnecessary noise.

So far this book has tried to impart the techniques needed to find the way with confidence across unfamiliar countryside. But this is only half the story. The ability to plan attractive walks must be acquired too if your new-found expertise is to get free rein.

Far from being a chore, the planning process adds to the richness of walking. From poring over the maps of an area the night before to work out a route, until afterwards when muddy boots have been washed and body is soaked in a hot bath, you can relish the contentment that flows from completing a walk of your own creation.

What sort of walk do you want?

Nobody wants it to seem like a military operation to plan and take a walk – after all we only want to go out and enjoy ourselves – but even so, it does help to give some thought to the task, starting with the aims the walk should fulfil. These will help you choose your route.

First and foremost, how long should the walk last for? Is it to be a two-hour-long afternoon stroll or do you want to spend the whole day in getting to know a new piece of scenery? What is the most that the stamina of your party can cope with? Obviously, the walk must be planned to fall within limits.

Then there are other factors to consider, not all of which will apply every time. You will want to:

- *Decide if there is a specific place the walk should visit.*
- *Decide on the format: circular, linear or out-and-back. Your mode of transport will influence this choice.*
- *Follow footpaths with as little road work as possible.*
- *Choose the paths with the best views.*
- *Keep away from noisy motorways or main roads.*
- *Include pleasant villages and visit (or avoid?) popular beauty spots.*
- *Choose some walking in woods, but not too much.*
- *Choose a route within the navigator's competence.*
- *Keep within the party's limit of hill climbing (amount, steepness).*

"In the South Pennines near Holme."

- *If very windy, keep in the shelter of woods or hills.*
- *Have shortening possibilities and bad weather alternatives.*
- *In winter, plan to return well before nightfall.*
  Other factors can be added that are important to you.

The planning process

Having an idea of the sort of walk you want and where it will be, and having either the Landranger, Explorer or Outdoor Leisure map to hand, or possibly maps of both scales, what is the precise planning process?

There are four steps:

Step 1. Look for attractive stretches of path.

First you will have to form an overall feel for what your chosen area is like to walk, as described in page 36. Then home in on the best paths which could become the highlights of the walk – high hillside paths with views, attractive-looking villages, riverside paths – whatever looks specially appealing.

Step 2. Select from these stretches, joining them together to make a route.

Now the architecture of the walk, its overall make-up, is decided, and at the same time an attempt is made to devise a walk that is of the right length which also satisfies the aims you have set. With experience you will get a feel for the length of route on the map that suits you.

Step 3. Assess this route against your aims.

Now make certain the route has the right length, and that it will provide the experience you want from it.

Step 4. If some aims are not met, adjust the route.

If it's too long, find a short cut. Perhaps one part is too steep, so find a way round that stretch. Repeat steps 3 and 4 until the route is satisfactory. The practicalities of checking a route for distance and time are now examined, followed by an example of planning a walk in West Sussex.

The last thing you want on a planned walk is to have to make an unexpected detour! You may well be confronted by white signs declaring private property etc which seem daunting, even misleading, but a wooden public footpath signpost proves you have every right to walk down this drive.

Measuring the distance

Walks usually take a tortuous route across the map, making measurement of their length something of a problem. We are talking here about measuring the length of a whole walk, usually a distance of more than three kilometres, so the methods of judging short distances mentioned on page 63 won't work. Here are the most common ways of measuring the length of a walk:

By string*. Accumulate the length of the route on a piece of thin string by putting its end on the start of the route. Then lay the string over the route, matching its every twist and turn, until the end of the route is reached. Straighten out the measured length of string and lay it over a nearby set of grid squares to find its length in kilometres, estimating the number of tenths of the incomplete kilometre. You could instead use the scale line at the foot of the map which gives miles as well as kilometres.*

By eye*. A rough estimate can be quickly obtained by comparing the route with the grid squares it crosses, counting the kilometres along the walk's length. The diagonal of a grid square is about 1.5 kilometres long. This is the best method to use during a walk, should you have to re-plan midway round.*

By map measurer *(or opsiometer). If you expect to do a lot of planning, you may wish to buy one of these clever gadgets. Having first set the instrument to zero, track its little wheel along the intended route on the map; the wheel causes a pointer to move over a dial, calibrated for a number of different map scales. The distance can then be read off from where the pointer lies on the dial, against the map scale you are using (1:25,000 for Explorer or 1:50,000 for Landranger).*

If the correct scale is not present on your instrument, do not despair; having measured the route, simply run the instrument back across the grid lines in a straight line until the pointer reaches zero again. The route distance in kilometres is given by the number of grid squares crossed as you 'unwind' the pointer.

Opsiometer. The photo shows the instrument having measured a distance of 8km from a map scale 1:25,000.

If the farmer has put a bull with cows into a field crossed by a public path, then the odds are that it is from a beef breed which is permitted. This one looks docile enough. See page 17 'Rules for using Rights of Way'.

Distance for everyday walking

For everyday walking in your home territory, distance might be all you need for assessing a walk; there might be no need to convert the distance into time required because you get to know the distance that suits you best, be it 16km for a fairly stretching all day walk or just 6km for your habitual afternoon stroll. Having measured your new route, you will know whether it will do, or needs to be adjusted for length. However, if you are walking in a hilly area, particularly if it is unfamiliar, then to be sure of not biting off more than you can chew – you should also work out the walk's timings.

Your walking speed

Before working out the walk time, first you need to judge your speed of walking. Typically, an energetic fit person will be able to make 6 km per hour over good level country footpaths whilst a mixed group of ramblers with some young children might walk at an average of only 2 km/hr. Between these extremes, most people average between 3 and 4 km/hr. These speeds imply continuous progress, i.e. no stops, include the time taken in getting over stiles and assume 'average' terrain underfoot. On any particular day, the walk you are planning might not be 'normal'; special factors may oblige you to increase, or more likely, decrease the speed you use to plan the walk. Such factors are:

- *Rough terrain or off-path walking.*
- *Snow, mud, wind or other weather conditions.*
- *Heavy loads to carry.*
- *Large group needing time to cross stiles, etc.*

Timing the walk

Now you have a walk length in kilometres and an average speed. How long will the walk last? Well, this should be a simple sum, but those people whose arithmetic is perhaps not what it used to be might

"The Goyt valley, Derbyshire."

need a little help. If, conveniently, your average walk speed is 3, 4 or 5 km/hr then you allow 20, 15 or 12 minutes per km, respectively, an easy calculation. But what if your speed is, say, 3.5 km/hr? Help is at hand in the form of the graph, which lets you make a direct read out.

The example (red arrows) works out the walk time for a 13km walk at 3.5 km/hr.
Answer: 3 hours 40 minutes.

Use the graph to calculate the walk time of your own walks. If the walk is longer than the graph can cope with, split the walk and add the times of the separate parts.

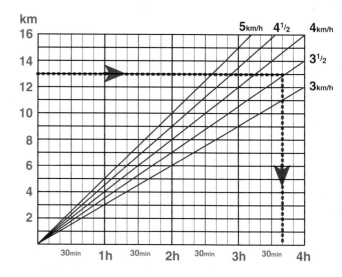

*Having calculated the walking time (**Walk**), some additions must be made for **Stops** (I allow 15mins each half day plus 45mins for lunch), for **Hills** (see below), and a bit extra for the unexpected **Just in Case!** For example:*

*   **Walk** 4h 50min. **Hills** 35min. **Stops** (lunch plus breaks) 1h 15min. **Just in Case** 20min. **Total 7 hours.**

Climbing hills

Most good walks have hills to climb. The fact that they slow you down was recognised many years ago by an exceedingly fit Scotsman called Naismith, who liked to tramp the Highlands. When planning his outings he would allow an hour for each 3 miles covered, a pretty fair pace considering the terrain plus, interestingly enough to us now, an extra half hour for each 1000 feet climbed. This is known as Naismith's Rule and is still widely used. In the hilly parts of the country it remains as good a rule of thumb as any. The '3 miles per hour'

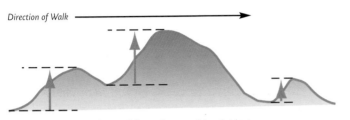

Direction of Walk ➝

Total height ascended on walk = sum of three heights in orange.

aspect we have already covered under **Walk**, but not the climbing. Converted to metric values, Naismith's Rule states:

'Allow 30 minutes extra for each 300m of ascent'.

When planning a walk using a map with a 10m contour interval (e.g. Landranger), the rule converts handily to: 'allow one minute extra for each contour line crossed when ascending'. Note that the rule applies only to those parts of the route that ascend - see diagram above – which means taking care to read the contours accurately.

As for descents, the theory is that on average they do not affect your speed. In general this is true, but lengthy steep descents require an extra time allowance. Half the amount allowed for the ascent would seem reasonable, or more in extreme circumstances.

If a walk contains no lengthy climbs, it over-eggs the pudding to apply Naismith's Rule rigorously. You can spend too much time looking at a lot of fiddly contours, ending up with just a few minutes being added to the walk time. Where the hills never top 250m just use your judgement. If the route seems to be crossing lots of contours, simply add 15 minutes each half day to compensate.

Landranger 148

Calculating the ascent:

This walk starts at spot height 356 and goes clockwise. There are three ascents:

1. **From A to B** the lowest point is say 350, the highest at point B is 520 = 170m.

2. **From C to D** the lowest point is on the 350 contour, the highest on the 470 = 120m.

3. **From E to F** counting contours between the two points, seven lines crossed = 70m.

Total ascent is 360m, allow 36min for Hills.

"Bignor Hill."

Planning in practice

Wanting an all-day walk in West Sussex, the village of Sutton caught my eye, with its pub as a possibility for lunch. We like to walk about 12 to 14km (about 8 miles) and noticing also the Roman Villa, we thought we would visit that too, which would add an hour to the walk. We normally do a circular walk getting to the start by car, and walk at 4 km/hour. With this summary of our aims for the walk, how does the planning work out?

1. Look for attractive stretches of path.

Disregarding the coloured routes on the map for now, the overall shape of this piece of countryside is of gently undulating land to the the north east, studded with enticing villages. Rising to the south and west, the rolling hills of the South Downs provide an intriguing contrast. There is a fine network of paths between the villages; a good set of tracks

joining the crests of the Downs, and a choice of paths up the steep
slope from the villages up to the crest tracks. All these paths look good
to walk, but a selection of all types would seem to be ideal.

2. Select from these stretches, joining them to make up a route.
*If we start from the car park to the south (by point 208), we can
construct a route that takes in the Roman Villa and still*

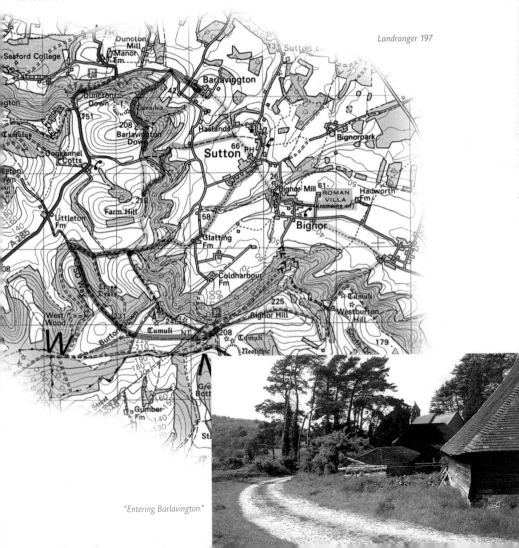

Landranger 197

"Entering Barlavington."

gives a good walk before lunch at the pub in Sutton. Follow the route highlighted in yellow, via Bignor Hill and by Westburton Hill.

For the afternoon, a return along the crest of the downs from Barlavington Down in the north-west would seem ideal, and this can take us to the village of Barlavington too. The possible afternoon route continues in yellow.

Final timings

Walk 14km @ 4km/hr = 3h30min
Villa Stop 1h
Lunch stop 45min
pm Stop 15min
Hills 15min*
Just In Case 15min
TOTAL 6h.

Starting at 10am, we get back to the car park at 4pm.

* Note As none of the hills exceeds 250m we need only add 15min per half day if the walk looks hilly.
The morning is mostly downhill, so add nothing then. The afternoon looks decidedly hilly so add the allowance.

(If Naismith had been applied in the afternoon, with 27 contour lines ascended, 27 mins should have been added. Thus we underestimated the walk time by 12mins using our rule of thumb.)

3. Assess this route against your aims.

Paths from the lowland area, the Downs and the slopes between them are all included, and we visit three of these attractive small villages. But measuring the length of the yellow route, it comes to 11km, just a little short for our purposes. It does include the pub, but what about the time we arrive there? It's 6km from the car park to the pub (90mins walking) and we must allow 1hr for the visit to the villa, making 2.5 hours altogether. If we plan to start from the car park at 10am we should reach the pub at a timely 12.30pm.

4. If some aims are not met, adjust the route.

The route for the afternoon needs to be made longer. Examination of the map reveals two possible extensions, shown in red – beyond Barlavington, adding 1km – and diverting south to join the South Downs Way for a stretch, adding 2km. With both extensions the walk becomes 14km long. The short cuts in blue are there to be taken if the weather deteriorates.

Scale of map for planning

Walkers seem equally divided as to which map is easier to use for planning a walk, 1:25,000 or 1:50,000. I prefer the 1:50,000 as it gives a better overview of the whole route; on 1:25,000 maps walks cover such a large area of paper that you easily lose the thread of where you want to go.

On Landranger maps the all-important relief stands out better because the contour lines are printed in a darker shade of brown.

"Walking in the South Pennines above Holme."

It helps to have the Explorer at hand, to check whether a complicated bit of route is possible to walk by path, or whether field boundaries might bar progress in open country. The 1:25,000 map, perhaps crucially, can confirm the existence of footbridges where paths cross 'single-line' streams, something the 1:50,000 map is silent about.

Can walks taken from the map be trusted?

A problem with planning solely from the map is that you cannot be sure paths are open on the ground. They are likely to be all right in popular walking areas, but in deeper countryside some paths might have fallen into disuse or be blocked. In an area new to you, plan those first walks fairly conservatively, making them somewhat shorter than normal, and with some alternatives up your sleeve, in case a path won't 'go'.

You can use parts of local guide book walks (which should have been checked by the author), if there are any, transferring their described route to the map. Bridleways and tracks might be preferred to footpaths, as these seem to be more reliable. After the first day or so in your new neighbourhood you will learn its quirks and will be able to plan accordingly.

Above all, have confidence that the walks you plan from the map will be most enjoyable. Guide book writers have no mystical advantage – after all they do no more than work out a route from the map. Just occasionally you will be disappointed with parts of a route, maybe the path that gave rise to such high hopes of exhilarating views turns out to be an ancient sunken track with thickly growing trees on either side. Fortunately the reverse is true much more often. Your routes reveal pleasant surprises of unexpected views, banks of flowers, interesting old barns and delightful villages, detail that could only have been guessed at from the map. And every map walk is uniquely yours!

"There is de facto acceptance of access on these south Snowdonia hills. Cador Idris looms on the horizon."

Dartmoor, Snowdonia, the Lake District and the Scottish Highlands;
these names and many more evoke images of wild and beautiful
scenery. They are magnificent places to walk in, but what marks out
navigation in such areas? Away from cultivated valleys, two factors
stand out:

- *A lack of man-made features to navigate by.*
- *The risk of mist obscuring the view.*

Either one of the above factors on its own is easy enough to cope with.
If you can interpret contours well, you will find your way easily enough
over all but the most featureless moors in good weather. And if the mist does come down, few problems will be encountered in the lowlands where the next building, footpath junction or corner of woodland can still be seen through the gloom. Problems set in when the two factors come together: featureless ground in the mist. Since all you can see as you walk is a changing circle of dripping

All you can see in mist is a changing circle of dripping grass and rock.

grass or rock, you risk losing your bearings and your navigational skills are tested to the full.

Skills and techniques

The process of navigating across a stretch of wild country is similar
to that described in Chapter 5, in that you move across the country in
a series of legs. With the larger scale of the landscape and fewer
mapped details, the legs tend to become somewhat fewer and longer,

**Good hill navigation is based on
good map reading**

*Just as with navigating over lowland
country, it is crucial to regard basic
map reading skill as fundamental to
good hill navigation, as it is this which
lets you make the positive fixes needed
for tracking your progress on the map.
Compass work, pacing and even
nowadays the GPS, useful though they
are, should all be treated as a back up
to good map skills.*

*but the essential process is the same. The difference comes in the
techniques for carrying out the process and how they are used:*

- *More skill is needed with contours and compass.*
- *You need to assemble a toolkit of special techniques from which to
pick and choose according to circumstances.*

*After a comment on the special case of walking on good hill paths,
with an example, this chapter is divided into four sections:*

SECTION 1 **TECHNIQUES**

SECTION 2 **PLANNING**

SECTION 3 **ON-THE-DAY NAVIGATION**

SECTION 4 **TECHNICAL AIDS**

Navigating on good hill paths

*In England and Wales, nine tenths of all hill and moorland walking
is done on well marked footpaths, indeed so well marked in the popular
walking areas that they can suffer from overuse. Such paths should be
easy enough to follow on a clear day but when the mist comes down
you lose sight of the big picture thereby increasing the chance of
missing a path or of taking the wrong one. To be on the safe side in
poor visibility, some hill navigational skills are needed even if you intend
to stick to the beaten track.*

*Having said that, the best way of cutting your teeth on hill
navigation is to do routes in mist on the good path network you can be
sure to find in a well-walked place, such as the Lake District.
Since you will be staying on paths, your main tasks are to be sure
always to pick the right path at junctions, and to keep track of your
position as you go. This will require quite an intensive level
of concentration, particularly when making route choices, with contour
work and simple compass techniques being the key.*

*But at the end of the day it's a great feeling to have followed
a hill walk accurately in mist.*

"Swirl How." Photo John Dawson

Outdoor Leisure 6

Navigating on good paths in mist

*To get the feel for such a walk, let's take the yellow route from point **A** to Swirl How at **F**.*

*From **A** we need to get up first to Wetherlam Edge to our SW, but the right of way path going directly there (arrowed) is probably not walked on the ground as there is no black-dashed line. Better to take the marked path going to the mine workings at **B**.*

*From **B** turning left at the mine, the path climbs straight up the slope and then veers right, and then 400m from the mine it turns sharp left. This description should suffice to recognise the path correctly on the ground.*

*At **C** we have reached the ridge and have picked up a well worn path. We turn right and ascend to the summit of Wetherlam. The path keeps at first to the right of the crest of the ridge. Getting to a summit is usually simple as all routes lead there by going up.*

But at D which is our route down from the top?

When choosing the correct path from a summit in mist it is essential to confirm the choice by compass, as it is astonishingly easy to become disoriented on a summit. In our case we ignore the green dashes of the right of way path (and the solid green line of the old-style National Trust boundary). The little black dashes mark our path on the ground. It goes due west initially, so we use compass direction to fix on this path. It descends due west for 200m to a flatter bit, and then traverses the northern slopes of Black Sails (slope up to the left), before descending to the saddle Swirl Hause.

*At **E** we should see a gully with stream going down left and a wider slope descending right. But we just ascend the ridge ahead up to the summit of Swirl How.*

Contour interpretation

Typically, even the remotest wild areas in England and Wales are not completely devoid of man-made features, but they could well be widely scattered. When route finding, you will find yourself placing great store by the occasional lone building, such as a barn or shooting hut; woods and forests are very helpful as landmarks and, if you have the 1:25,000 map, you will look out for walls and fences. Also footpaths and tracks are navigational features in their own right.

But, even with a sprinkling of these features and certainly if there are none, you need to have skill in interpreting contours (and you will use streams and rock markings too), as the relief often provides the only clues for fixing position. With some practice, you will be able to translate the pattern of contours in the map into a number of separate features that you can use to navigate by.

Not only are such features perhaps the only ones available to you in some remote locations, they are always very reliable, as they do not change with time. The features are those already described in Chapter 2, but they need to be used with subtlety, looking at landforms of all sizes. Check that you are able to recognise the following, both as large and small features:

- Spurs and ridges.
- Valleys and their smaller cousins, re-entrants.
- Separate hill tops.
- Saddles (also called a col, or in the Lake District, a hause).
- Slopes of differing steepness.
- Slopes too steep to walk safely.
- Concave and convex slopes.
- Rock markings.
- Cliffs and outcrops.

The Compass

In poor visibility on hill or moorland, the compass becomes an essential tool. It is used primarily to define direction of travel but it has other uses that can be brought into play from time to time. Essentially, there are two broad approaches, **map to ground** *and* **ground to map**, *each having a number of techniques.*

Compass: map to ground

- *Point path direction.*
- *Take and follow a bearing.*

  The first two techniques cover 95% compass usage, but you can also:
- *Take a back bearing.*
- *Identify a distant landmark on the ground.*

Compass: ground to map

- *Draw position line on the map.*
- *Direction of slope*
- *Identify distant landmark on map*

  These techniques are much less often used.

Point path direction

This is technique is covered in Chapter 6, 'The Compass' on page 73. Although the example points a path direction in woodland the same method applies to hill and moorland paths.

Take and follow a bearing

This is the classical use of a compass, for plotting a course across trackless open ground. When visibility is severely reduced as in mist, at night or in a forest, distant landmarks can no longer be seen and the

A contour quiz

The photo and map show a remote part of the northern Lake District. The Outdoor Leisure map has a contour interval of 10m. Can you use your contour interpretation skills to answer these questions?

1. *Which of tops* **A**, **B**, **C** *and* **D** *are visible, and which is the highest?*
2. *Which of streams* **1**, **2**, **3** *and* **4** *cannot be seen, and why?*
3. *What is the landform* **F–F**?
4. *What kind of slopes are* **A–E** *and* **G–G**?
5. *Pick out in both the photograph and map the isolated hillock in the foreground and the levelled-out spur behind it. What is the height of the ring contour marking the hillock?*
6. *Going from* **A** *to* **D** *via* **B** *and* **C**, *work out the distance, height gain and time by Naismith. (Although it is probably rather fast for this terrain, assume 4km/hr walking speed).*

Answers

1. *Only B can be seen, C is highest.*
2. *Stream 4 is hidden behind the broad flank of hill D.*
3. *A valley (or re-entrant).*
4. *A–E convex and G–G concave.*
5. *340m.*
6. *Distance. 2.5km, Height gain. 200m, Time. 2.5x15 minutes per km =37.5 minutes for the horizontal walking, plus 20 minutes for the ascent = 57.5 minutes total, say 1 hour in total.*

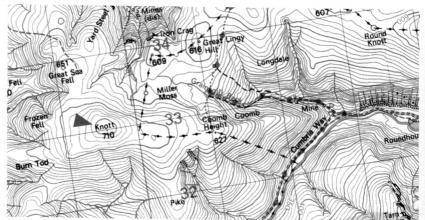

Landranger 90

compass might be the only means of accurate direction finding. In the northern Lake District hills you have reached the summit of Knott, featureless except for the cairn, and now cloud has descended. You wish to get off as easily as possible, and have chosen to take the 'spur 'descending from Coomb Height to the road in the valley to the east. How do you take the bearing to Coomb Height and then walk there?

Take the bearing using Steps A to C as described on the opposite page, and then walk the bearing using the method below. When following a long leg in mist, take a careful sighting at the start of the leg, picking out clearly defined objects in line with the direction of travel, e.g. a tree, a rock, a tuft of grass even. It should be as far away as possible, but not so far that you could lose sight of it, especially in swirling mist or cloud, as you walk towards it.

Having fixed on the object, put the compass away and walk up to it. Once the object is reached, repeat the process keeping the compass set to the same bearing, picking out another object on this bearing. Continue from point to point in this way until you reach your objective.

On closer examination...

Looking more closely at the map, the spur descending from Coomb Height to the road becomes very steep lower down. It would be better to leave Coomb Height to the north and pick up the valley path that leads past the mine. A longer but safer route.

Step A

Place the compass on the map with an edge of the base aligned from Knott to Coombe Height, with the direction of travel arrow pointing toward Coombe Height.

Step B

Holding the base firm, turn the housing round until the north lines are parallel with north-pointing grid lines, with the north arrow pointing to north on the map.

Step C

Take the compass off the map. Holding the compass (see page 73, step C), turn your whole body round until the needle lines up with the north arrow (red on red).

The direction of travel arrow now points along the line of the route you should take.

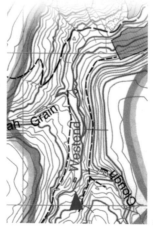

Harvey Superwalker "Dark Peak"

Take a back bearing

This technique is used if you wish to retrace your steps, having started out on a leg, or if you want to check your accuracy of travel on a leg when you can still see where you started out from.

Simply hold the compass with the base pointing away from you with the bearing set as before. Then turn your whole body round until the needle lines up, so that the white end of the needle is on the north arrow (white on red). You are now pointing back the way you came.

Identify a distant landmark on the ground

You have a landmark on the map, and you want to know which it is on the ground. Take its bearing with the compass from your current position on the map. Step C (page 101) will cause the compass to point to it on the ground. Use your map reading skills to identify the particular landmark on this line.

Now the techniques working from ground to map:

You will find yourself placing great store by the occasional lone building to confirm your location.

This ruined sheepfold (a small oblong on the map just above the arrow) pinpoints your position even if in this case the contour pattern should be sufficient on its own.

Draw position line on the map

*You are uncertain of your current position but can see a distant feature identifiable both on the ground and map. Take a bearing from the feature and use this to define a **position line** that runs from the distant feature. Your current position must be at some point along this line.*

This technique works well when you are walking on a long linear feature such as a ridge or the edge of a forest (as in the example below),

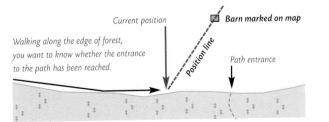

Current position

Barn marked on map

Walking along the edge of forest, you want to know whether the entrance to the path has been reached.

Position line

Path entrance

Position Line in practice.

*We have left Crag Hill
to walk over Sail, and want to know
how far we have progressed. A break in
the clouds reveals the mine in the valley
below to our left.
So we take out our compass and take
the bearing of the mine (Step A)
and draw the position line (StepB).*

but do not know how far you have travelled along it. Perhaps a momentary parting of the clouds gives a glimpse of a recognisable hill, a remote barn or a stream junction. By taking the bearing from the feature, you can draw the position line on the map, and so can pinpoint your position at the spot where it intersects with the linear feature.

Step A

Take the bearing of the mine by:

1. Pointing the direction of travel arrow at the mine and
2. Rotating the housing until the north arrow is lined up with the needle.

Then (if you wish) allow for magnetic variation by subtracting. Here the magnetic bearing is 16°. Subtract 4° variation to give 12° grid.

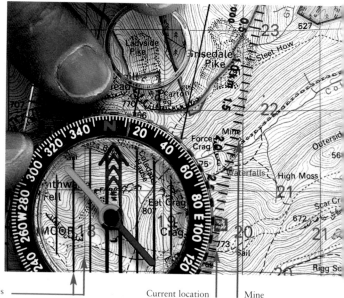

North lines parallel to map grid lines ——————— Current location | Mine

Landranger 90

Direction of slope

Once again you are uncertain of your position in the mist and are looking for clues. If you can see enough through the mist to be sure that the slope about you falls in a consistent direction, then you can take the bearing of the fall line (i.e. the line directly down the slope) and transfer that direction to the map.

Then your position on the map can only be where contour lines run at right angles to this direction. Almost certainly, few places of the area in which you could be will have this slope direction, thus narrowing down possibilities. The beauty of this method is that it can be done in mist.

The same technique can be used with the direction of a stream or other linear feature such as a wall, a path or the edge of a wood, to locate yourself on the particular stream etc. having that direction.

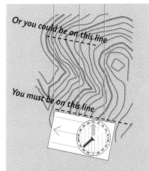

Direction of Slope

Having taken the bearing of the fall line down the slope, place the compass on map and rotate the whole compass until the north lines are aligned with the north pointing grid lines. (Do not adjust the housing).

Hold the compass in this orientation, move it over the map until you find a place or places where the contour lines intersect the edge of the compass at right angles.

Your position should be on one of these places.

Step B

Having taken the bearing (12° grid in this case) put the compass on the map with an edge of the baseplate on the distant object (the Mine).

Now pivot the compass edge about the Mine until the north lines on the compass are aligned with the north grid lines (north arrow must also be pointing north on the map).

Our position is now somewhere on the edge of the compass – i.e. the position line. Since in this case we know we are on the Crag Hill – Sail ridge, we must be at the arrowed point left.

Identify distant landmark on map

In clear weather you know where you are and wish to identify on the map a distant hill top, cliff or other feature. Take the bearing of the distant feature and transfer the position line to the map. In this case make the position line run through your current position. The distant

"The Rhinogs rise to the left here in Snowdonia."

If you were to take position lines from two or even three points, the point at which they intersect would give your position. This is the famous technique of resection.

Alas, when you don't know where you are, the visibility is nearly always so poor that you cannot identify three distant points, so in practice resection is hardly ever used.

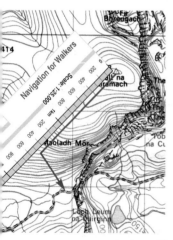

Landranger 23

It's misty.

The direct path from the trig point to the car goes over steep cliffs, so to be safe a dog-leg route is needed.

The first part needs to be timed, to know when it is safe to turn left, taking a second bearing down to the car. How long is the first leg?

The scale shows 1.5km.

At 4km/hr (the going underfoot is good and the slope is not steep) this will take 22.5mins.

feature then lies somewhere along this line on the map unless, of course, it is so far away as to be off the edge of the map.

Measuring distance on the ground

As far as possible you will want to track your position on the ground as you walk by means of features seen on both map and ground.

If landforms exist, then you should be able to make out the relief and interpret this on the map by the contours. Alas, particularly in a forest or in mist, even this method can sometimes break down and you find that you just cannot see enough. Then you will have to resort to using the compass for direction and some form of measurement to keep track of how far you have walked.

The first step is to measure from the map the distance to your next check point. Either use a special scale (such as the one on the last page of the book), or use the millimetre scale on your compass. Each millimetre is worth 25m on a scale of 1:25,000 or 50m on 1:50,000. (See page 63.)

The best ways of measuring a distance out on the ground are by **pacing** or by **timing**. There is a rule of thumb: for short distances up to about 400 metres use pacing; for longer distances use timing.

Pacing

You need to know how many double paces you take for 100 metres. Double pacing means that you count your left foot hitting the ground (or right foot) and is better than single pacing as only half the counting is needed. A person of average stature might take 65 double paces but you need to work out your own pace count on a measured 100m stretch.

Supposing you have measured 270m for a leg, the way to pace it out it is to count two lots of 65 paces (or whatever your personal count is) to give 200m and then to estimate the final 70m as 7/10ths of 65 = 45 paces. Slopes up or down or poor conditions underfoot require an

Check for Steepness

In a remote part of North Wales this mountain has de facto right of access. It may be climbed easily on its western and northern slopes. But to the S and E, some intermediate contours are missing, indicating steep slopes. (On Landranger maps when a slope is 1 in 3 or steeper, the OS omits intermediate contours, but the thicker index contours will always be present.)

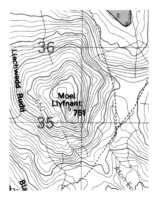

adjustment to increase the number of paces per 100m. Steep slopes shorten your stride dramatically.

Timing

You need to estimate your walking speed in km/hr. for the leg being measured. Then you can work out how many minutes you need to allow for the distance to be travelled. At 4 km/hr., an 'average' speed, it takes 1.5 minutes to cover each 100 metres, so a leg of 700m will take 10.5 minutes at this speed. Once again, whatever your usual walking speed, it is greatly affected by slopes, poor conditions underfoot and other factors, so you will have to adjust accordingly.

As you will probably have guessed already, it is often very difficult to achieve a high level of accuracy with these forms of distance measurement. A good level track eases the task but if there are slopes, snow, undergrowth or many rocks, then you will not be doing badly if you stay within a 20% error level. High wind and heavy loads affect measurement, too. For all the inaccuracy, it is always much better to measure than to guess.

SECTION 2 **PLANNING**

In some ways you will give less attention to planning a hill walk before setting out, but other crucial matters will demand more attention, compared with an outing in the lowlands.

Once you leave the security of footpaths, only a broad-brush route choice is needed before setting out, since the finer points will be decided as you start each new leg, and can see what you are faced with. Often you will not be able to work out the details of a route until you are on the walk and can actually see the terrain ahead. 'That scree looks wearisome to ascend, but we can take the grassy slope to the left of that buttress,' or 'The path curving round to the right we planned to take is OK, but the rocky spur ahead looks inviting, so we'll take that.'

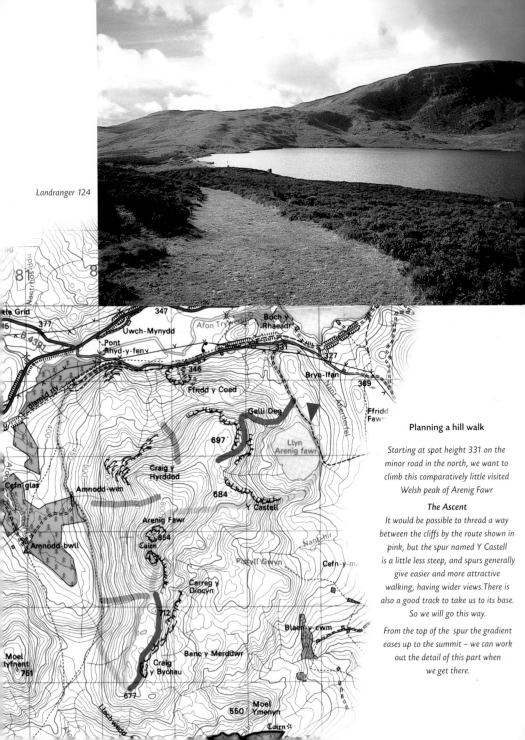

Landranger 124

Planning a hill walk

Starting at spot height 331 on the minor road in the north, we want to climb this comparatively little visited Welsh peak of Arenig Fawr

The Ascent

It would be possible to thread a way between the cliffs by the route shown in pink, but the spur named Y Castell is a little less steep, and spurs generally give easier and more attractive walking, having wider views. There is also a good track to take us to its base. So we will go this way.

From the top of the spur the gradient eases up to the summit – we can work out the detail of this part when we get there.

Looking across Llyn Arenig Fawr to our ascent route up Y Castell.

The Descent

It would be possible to take any of the three blue routes for a direct descent. They are on the borderline of acceptable steepness but each would be very wearisome as they descend steeply a very long way.
Other direct ways are too steep. Better is to go south to spot height 677, because there will be a fine view south from there and it is easy from there to pick up the valley footpath for the return. The way over the flat boggy part by pink or yellow route can be worked out after inspecting it on the descent from the top.

How long will it take?

Measuring its length at 14km, and assuming a speed of 3.5km/hr over quite a lot of rough ground, the chart on page 86 gives a **Walk** *time of 4 hours. Add to this:*
Ascent of (854-331=523m),
say 52mins for **Hills***;*
plus 1h15mins for **Stops***;*
plus 20mins **Just in Case**
TOTAL 6h 27mins*.*

Escape Routes

There are no feasible midway escapes, so it's a matter of turning back or pressing on. This should be no problem as the distance on the mountain itself is quite short.

Access

Although there is no formal agreement, de facto access exists, confirmed by local enquiries. The Outdoor Leisure map shows a couple of fences to be crossed, but the ranger confirmed the existence of stiles for our route.

The planning done before the walk can use the process set out in Chapter 7, but with these differences:

- **Check route timing**. You will calculate the duration of the walk, to be sure it can be finished within the time and stamina you have, and especially in winter before nightfall. In the hills it is essential to use Naismith to allow for height gain.

- **Check route steepness**. Examine the route critically on the map, checking that no section is too steep. It's all too easy to include without realising it even a small section where the contour lines are bunched too closely together for comfort. The Landranger map is usually best for this check. In Scotland, see what the Scottish Mountaineering Club Regional (or Munro) Guide has to say about your route. These guides are a mine of practical information on the main routes up Scottish hills.

- **Check for field boundaries**. If you are going off-path be sure by checking locally you have right of access to the land. And use the 1:25,000 map to check that you will not need to climb over fences or walls.

- **Devise escape routes**. In case the weather turns nasty or your party wants to cut the outing short, it is crucial to have one or two escape routes up your sleeve. One alternative might simply be 'turn back'.

- **Ensure your route is navigable**. If you intend going off path, or you mistrust the quality of the paths in your area, then it makes sense to anticipate the mist coming down. Would you be able to navigate the route accurately enough then? To make this check, rehearse the more detailed route-finding decisions you would make on the walk.

- **Work out crucial bearings beforehand**. When planning your route note particular bearings such as the descents from summits to have ready on the hill when needed. It is easier to do this in the warmth of home than in a howling gale on the hill.

Route cards

To ensure good planning, youth organisations insist that their parties prepare a route card for each outing. This documents the grid

Landranger 147

Wanting to climb from the bridge at **A** to the hilltop at **B**, you could climb up directly, though it would be very steep.

How much better to take the gentle old quarry track to the disused quarry, and walk on the level from there to the hilltop. Much longer in distance, but maybe not in time, and much more pleasant.

Be prepared

Besides time spent beforehand on the formal process of planning your expedition, it's worth just looking at and learning the route by reading the map.

Get to know the structure of the walk – the ascents, peaks to be visited and what the descents will look like. You can form a picture of the tricky points of the route, and think through some strategies for dealing with them. That way the decisions on the day will come all the more easily.

Get a drink of whatever takes your fancy, settle into an armchair, and enjoy the walk even before you have started.

references of the route, divided into between four and eight major legs, and gives the **Walk, Hills, Stops, Just in Case** times for each leg and the whole route. The party takes one copy and leaves another at base.

Private adult parties mostly do not bother with the formality of this, wanting anyway to be free to change plans as the day unfolds. There is normally little risk in this provided the party always walks cautiously and well within its capacity. On demanding excursions there is merit in doing the calculations of a route card to be sure of good planning. It must be a matter of choice whether you then leave it with a responsible person to raise the alarm if you do not return as planned. If you do this, it is of course essential to inform that person of a safe return.

SECTION 3 **ON-THE-DAY NAVIGATION**

As we have seen, the boundary between planning beforehand and on-the-day decisions is blurred. People with less experience tend to be more precise in the planning than old hands, who take a more relaxed approach. Either way, the principles guiding your route choices tend to be the same, whether they are the bigger decisions taken beforehand or the smaller ones made on the day.

The key to navigating a leg of your walk accurately, is to devise a strategy for it. To do this you will dip into your toolkit of techniques, picking out the ones best suited to the leg. The main compass and distance measurement techniques have been explained – here are more hints and tips.

Hints and tips

A longer route by path is often quicker and easier to follow than a shorter cross country route. Where the cut-off comes depends on the terrain. Cross country travel is easy over the short cropped grass of Bodmin Moor so here the advantage of taking a path is not great. The reverse is true in the Rhinog range in Wales where much of the terrain consists of boulders concealed by knee-high heather. You will scour the map for every path here.

A longer route on the level is often quicker and less tiring than a more direct route over hills and valleys. Keep a keen eye open for the number of contours your route crosses. Is there a flatter, possibly longer alternative? Mind you, the purpose of the walk may be to take in those attractive peaks.

Spurs and ridges often provide superior routes compared with valleys. The all-round views from a ridge are better than from the enclosed space of a valley. Spurs usually have shorter vegetation and fewer marshes compared with stream side routes which frequently run into broken ground and tangled vegetation, unless a path can be seen clearly.

Avoid off-path descents down convex slopes, unless you are quite sure of the ground. You cannot see from the top if there might be dangerously steep ground and, once there, there is always the temptation to try to find a way down, risking more trouble, rather than face the climb back up to look for another safer way.

Look on the map for linear features to navigate by. Obvious linear features (besides paths!) are field boundaries, edges of forests and streams. More subtle linear features can be discerned from the contours – ridges, spurs and valleys and even lines where the slope gets steeper, such as the rim of a plateau. Orienteers call such linear features 'handrails' when they are followed as part of a route. They come into their own in poor visibility.

When planning to cross featureless ground, try to end on a 'collecting feature.' This is another use of an obvious linear feature. If you need a compass bearing to cross featureless ground, the 'collecting feature' will tell you clearly that you have arrived, thereby avoiding the need to pace or time the distance. Once there, it might turn into your 'handrail'.

When taking a compass bearing to a specific point on a collecting feature, then 'aim off'. Maybe you are wanting to get to a bridge over a stream or the entrance of a path into a forest.

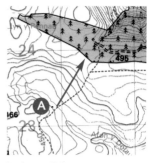

Landranger 125

Aiming Off

In mist, you have reached the stream at **A** but the path up the hillside to the wood has disappeared. You want to join the path through the wood. Rather than take a direct bearing, use your compass to follow the arrowed course.

When you hit the forest, you know to turn right. Even better, having turned right and getting to the angle in the wood, you know the path is only 100m further on.

As there can be no doubt about when you have reached the wood, there is no need to pace or time the distance.

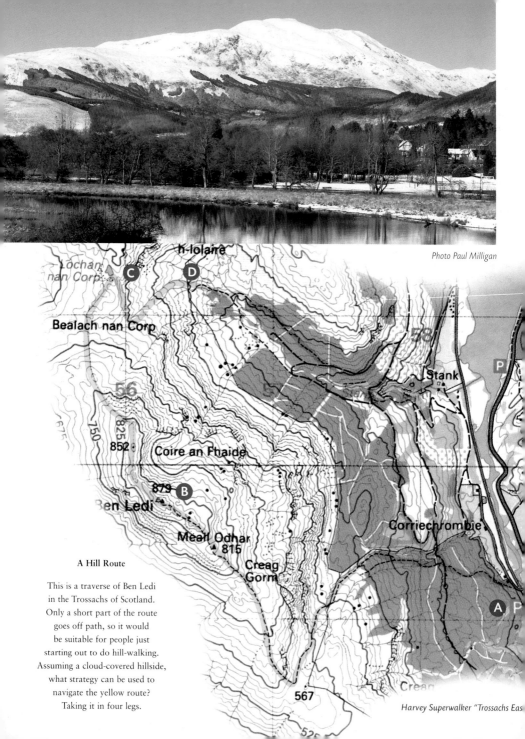

h-Iolaire

C D

Bealach nan Corp

Lochan
nan Corp

56

750

825

852   Coire an Fhaide

675

879 B

Ben Ledi

Meall Odhar
815

Creag
Gorm

567

Stank

P

Corriechrombie

A   P

Creag

A Hill Route

This is a traverse of Ben Ledi
in the Trossachs of Scotland.
Only a short part of the route
goes off path, so it would
be suitable for people just
starting out to do hill-walking.
Assuming a cloud-covered hillside,
what strategy can be used to
navigate the yellow route?
Taking it in four legs.

Harvey Superwalker "Trossachs Eas

From A to B

Starting from the car park to the east, the route to the summit is clear to navigate, as there is a well-used path, marked on the map, all the way to the summit (50mins).

From B to C

The path now ceases. The next target is the small lake Lochan nan Corp. For the first 600m it is a matter of continuing along the summit ridge, first north-west, then north, to the point where it falls away steeply ahead. From here remains of a boundary are shown on the map going NW then N all the way to the loch. If it is visible, it can be followed as a handrail all the way there. If not, the spur down to the NW should be taken (use a compass bearing to check direction) for 400m to where the slope lessens and a small hillock is reached. Now take a compass bearing to walk to the loch, 700m away. The important thing is to keep on the broad ridge.

From C to D

The route now descends east to a boundary wall and the start of a path, 550m away. But the direct route is too steep. So, walk on a bearing for 400m to the start of a stream (by the "C" of Corp), and then follow the stream down, keeping it to your left. In fact you will find yourself following a tiny spur. The path starts just below the boundary, where the stream is running due east.

From D to A

A succession of paths returns you to the car park.

Walk *Distance 11km. at 3km/hr*
=3h40mins
Hills *Climb (879-130)=750m*
=1h15mins
Stops *1h 15mins*
Just in Case *30mins*
TOTAL 6h 40mins

If you take a direct bearing to the point, once you reach the collecting feature you may not see the bridge or path entrance owing to inaccuracy in following the bearing, and then not know which way to turn. To avoid this, deliberately set a compass course 10° say, off to one side. Then, on reaching the collecting feature, you will know whether to turn left or right to walk to the point.

Look for ground features pointing to your position. To keep track of your position, one trick is to look out for features that point directly to where you find yourself. For example, you might see a stream flowing mainly straight pointing directly to you. If you can identify the same stretch of stream on the map, you know you are somewhere on the line it projects. This works also with two point objects lined up.

Be observant. The canny walker is constantly looking for better routes than the one planned:

● Now that the actual terrain is visible, is there an easier choice than the one chosen before the walk?

● Is the bit that looked tricky on the map all right, now that you can see it on the ground?

● Which is the next escape route?

● If you are going to return along the way you are going on now, glance back every so often to memorise the route.

● At the start of a circular walk, can you see the return route for later in the day? Will it 'go' all right, or would an alternative be better?

If mist descends. Note where you are, take an immediate compass bearing of the direction you are walking and note the time. The bearing will stand you in good stead for this leg, and the best way of keeping

> ### SAFETY WARNING
>
> The higher hills in the UK are hostile places in bad weather.
> If you are new to hillwalking it is important to understand that there is much more to staying safe than being able to navigate well, important though that is. You should get to know about equipment, food, party management, weather and many other matters before undertaking hazardous routes in the hills.
>
> Above all, navigation and the other factors take on a new level of seriousness in winter conditions.

A wall is a linear feature, obviously easy to follow in poor visibility. Equally the line of the rim of a steep slope can be pressed into service.

track of distance covered is by rough distance/time calculations, based on an estimate of your speed of walking.

The art of hill navigation

If you can apply these hints and tips and have skill in map reading, contour interpretation and compass work, then you have a bulging toolkit for the task of forging a route across moor and hill. For any one stretch you will use only a few of the tools but, as with any craft, there is a knack in selecting the best ones to solve the particular problems posed by the route.

Some people seem to have a flair for finding the most natural line and then navigating it in a sure but simple way. With practice and experience everyone can become competent enough to enjoy the special contentment of doing their own hill and moorland routes, even in poor visibility.

SECTION 4 **TECHNICAL AIDS**

Global positioning system (GPS)

These hand held electronic devices lock onto the signals from satellites orbiting the earth to give an accurate read-out of the user's current grid reference, height above sea level and bearing and distance to the next preset point on the route. Since May 2000 when an in-built 'fuzz factor' was removed by the US Department of Defense, position is given to an astonishing level of accuracy, i.e. to within about 20 metres.

In practice the process of getting a fix usually takes longer than reading the map, rendering the device unnecessary for normal footpath walking or when making way across open country in good visibility. The private walker might buy one out of curiosity, but I guess they will be seen as being more cumbersome and slower in use than the map if you are going to stick to paths in easy country.

However they offer much more in wild country when the mist has come down. Then the read-out of a grid reference and height can give great assurance if your tracking of position against map features has broken down. In particular, if you are making way to a certain point by compass bearing and distance, the GPS can help by pointing the direction even if you have been forced off course by the terrain (this feature works only when you are on the move) and by removing the need to estimate distance (the GPS always gives the current distance to go).

However it should be borne in mind that even if the GPS can tell you where you are, it offers no help in reading the map to choose a safe route to follow. You will still need all your map skills to do this, and good navigational skills to follow the route accurately. Without a good feel for a map and good contour interpretation, you will have difficulty in using the information given by the GPS and in checking that you have not made a gross error in entering the next waymark.

A modern twelve channel GPS will give a reasonable reading in light woodland, but will not work in dense forest or when hemmed in on both sides by high cliffs. It pays to input the waymarks you might use on the walk before setting off, as this is a painstaking process difficult to do on a rain-lashed hillside. As with any portable electronic device, you need to read the manual thoroughly, practice its use in easy conditions and take a spare set of batteries.

Global Positioning System

Altimeter

An altimeter provides an an additional check on location in poor visibility by giving your height. If it says you are at 870m, then you must be on or near the 870m contour on the map. Combined with other information, such as the knowledge you are ascending a particular spur, you might be able to fix your position.

A GPS receiver gives altitude, but a dedicated altimeter might be a preferable device to use, on account of price, size or convenience. Whereas a GPS uses satellite location which never varies, most altimeters rely on the reduction in air pressure which occurs as height is gained. A partially evacuated box flexes in sympathy with the changes in air pressure, providing movement which can be translated into a changing read-out. Since changing weather patterns also influence air pressure, to preserve accuracy an altimeter must be reset as often as possible on reaching points of known height. If the instrument was reset within the last hour or two, the reading will be tolerably accurate.

Other electronic devices

The advance of electronics and minitiarisation brings the possibility of combining a number of functions into small devices, even of wristwatch size. Electronic sensors can now measure these physical properties:

- position (by GPS as above)
- altitude and atmospheric pressure
- magnetic north, and thus compass direction
- number of paces (for distance measurement)
- temperature

Taken together with time, many combinations of function are possible, all built into a small instrument. With time these devices will improve and become easier to use. Are they the future? Or will you just stick with your trusty map and compass?

This wristwatch measures time, altitude, pressure and temperature.

"Here in deepest Wales the bridleway through the gate is in good working order, but the footpath up the steps into the forest is totally blocked, even though the green dashes are clearly visible on the map."

Pay Attention

Call me stupid, but this actually happened – we were at point **A** intending to walk up the main valley to point **C**. I had looked quickly at the map and thought the main track went straight on for us at point **B** taking us around the wiggle to continue up the main valley, so no map reading would be needed for some time. And there were fungi to collect!

At point **B** in fact the main track keeps left up the valley south of Houndtor Wood, and we walked up this unawares. At point **D** the track goes across the stream, but I knew we did not want to cross it (the main river I still thought), so we took a minor path ahead. This petered out at point **E** when I realised we were lost.

Then, after collecting our thoughts, and having lunch, a compass bearing along the valley told us we had veered off into the side valley, and we planned an escape from there.

It can happen to anyone, even the most expert. You have been walking gaily along, but a growing sense of doubt finally makes you stop and look at the map. You realise that you cannot pinpoint your position and have to admit you are lost. What can cause this?

Perhaps, if the process of getting lost is understood a little, on some occasions you will be able to take precautions.

There are a number of reasons.

The navigation is just too difficult. Maybe your route takes you through a sizeable forest and the tracks on the ground bear no apparent relationship to the map. Or mist has come down to obscure distant navigational marks. With experience, you learn your capability and the sorts of terrain which will be difficult to navigate and therefore best avoided. Until this knowledge is gained it pays to err on the safe side and plan routes you know you can find.

Lack of concentration. This is the most common reason for missing the way. You are enjoying the walk so much that you give too little thought to the map reading. Perhaps you looked at your route and decided that it was easy – 'just along this track, follow your nose for the next 2 miles till there is a bridge over the river'. But you didn't pick up the small detail that showed the main path veering left half way along, and a right turn that was needed to resume the general direction straight ahead. You can blame that engrossing conversation about oriental religions for taking your mind off the subject and you now realise that you have been going wrong for the last mile or so.

A small mistake becomes a big one. Perhaps you have just made a mistake like the last one without realising it and something stops you recognising the fact. You persist along the wrong way, convincing yourself that there is nothing wrong. You force the facts of the wrong route to fit the original route on the map. 'Maybe the path has been re-routed' or 'Yes, that is Ringwood Hill, even if it does seem too far off to the left'. It is amazing how the mind can suffer this self-deception. Only much later does the ghastly realisation seep in, you have been going wrong for a mile or more and now you are well and truly lost. It is rather pointless to advise you not to do this as nothing seems to

control your mind in such a situation. Perhaps it helps just a
little to realise that your mind can work in this peculiar way and try to
be honest with yourself. A sceptical approach will always pay.

How to re-locate

Orienteers use this more reassuring word, rather than finding yourself,
or getting unlost, as it is comforting to imply that you are just a little
mislaid, not completely up a creek.

So, you are lost. What should you do? Readers of 'Hitchhiker's
Guide to the Galaxy' will know the first bit of advice "Don't panic!"
Stop, have a drink, take a seat perhaps, and collect your thoughts.
Enlist the aid of a companion with whom to talk things through. Being
lost is a relative term. You may not be able to pinpoint your position,
but you know you are not in the next county, as that would be
impossible considering where the walk started. So, already you are
beginning to narrow down the possibilities. Now take this further.

Apply some logic to deciding the bounds of possibility to where you
are – decide on an **area of probability**. You can start from the point
where you last think you had made a good fix of position -
how long ago was that? How far could you have walked in the time
since then, maximum and minimum? What are the bounds of direction
of travel, the most left of your route, the most right? By applying these
thoughts you should be able to fix on an area of the map which in all
probability contains your current position. Now you can try to re-locate
by applying the following Plans A, B or C.

Plan A. Try to work out where you are now by looking more
closely about you and relating what you see to different points in your
area of probability:
● Set the map by compass and get another person to hold it in the
set position
● With the set map, try to identify features visible both on map
and ground and use these to work out where you are. If necessary walk

a short distance to get a better view. Which paths on the map have the same direction as the one you are on? Can you see the edge of a wood, or buildings that might be on the map?

● Bring into play features that you may hitherto have been ignoring. Perhaps you did not look at the contours. What are the slopes doing locally? In which direction do they fall?

Plan B. If Plan A fails, can you retrace your steps to the last identifiable point, and re-plan the route from there?

Plan C. In some circumstances, you can work out a route that will be satisfactory, no matter where you are in your area of probability. You might be in a forest which is not too dense. In open ground in mist, Plan C might be your only option. Here you look for a route to take you to a collecting feature that will let you relocate your position. A compass bearing to an adjoining track or other linear feature might meet this need. In open country you must make certain that, irrespective of where you are in your area of probability, your route will not take you into danger.

In conclusion

Skill with map and compass opens up the whole 120,000 miles long network of public footpaths (more in Scotland) that criss cross the country. By getting out into these paths and into open land where free access is possible, the unique delights of the British countryside are at your beck and call. Nowhere else on earth is the happy conjunction present of these elements: a landscape scaled to human proportions in which the scenery changes pleasingly as you walk; easy access from a public footpath network; and a full range of accurate easy-to-read maps. With a new prowess in map reading the countryside is yours.

You have taken the pink route from south east to north west. The weather has closed in, it's getting unpleasant and you have lost track of position. Using Plan C, any route off left will bring you to the safety of the road. Nowhere will you get onto slopes too steep for comfort and there are no cliffs.

Landranger 135

"The farmer has restored the line of the public path after ploughing and drilling by running a tractor along its length."

USEFUL ADDRESSES

Countryside Agency

John Dower House, Crescent Place,
Cheltenham,
Gloucestershire GL50 3RA
Tel: 01242 521381
Fax: 01242 584270
Web: www. countryside.gov.uk

*The government agency that works
to conserve and enhance the beauty of
the English countryside. It advises
government on such matters and has
special responsibility for National
Parks, Areas of Outstanding Natural
Beauty and National Trails.
You can obtain the very informative
booklet "Out in The Country – where
you can go and what you can do"
from Countryside Agency Publications
(tel: 0870 120 6466) free of charge,
quoting "CA9".*

Cordee

3A De Montfort Street,
Leicester LE1 7HD
Tel: 0116 254 3579
Fax: 0116 247 1176
Web: www.cordee.co.uk

*Specialist distributors and publishers
of outdoor books, guides and maps.
The web site lists the full range of titles
available, with prices, which may
then be obtained from a bookshop or
direct from Cordee if in difficulty.*

Harvey Maps

12–16 Main Street, Doune,
Perthshire FK16 6BJ
Tel: 01786 841202
Fax: 01786 841098
Web: www.harveymaps.co.uk

*Publishers of some 60 maps,
mainly of northern upland areas, but
increasingly from lowland England,
including some route maps of
National Trails. A map index is
available free of charge, or visit their
web site where maps may be inspected
and ordered.*

National Navigation Award Scheme

2 Greenway, Park Lane, Brocton,
Stafford ST17 0TS
Tel: 01785 662915
Web: www.nnas.org.uk

*The scheme sets standards for courses
and assessments of navigational skills,
at three levels – bronze, silver and
gold. The courses are run by affiliated
organisations, a list of whom may be
obtained from the scheme office,
together with explanatory leaflets.
If you want to consolidate and test
your skills, this scheme provides a
good way to do it. The NNAS also
offers a Young Navigator scheme,
which aims to put youngsters on the
right path by building up map and
compass skills. The Young Navigator
booklet and teacher's starter pack is
available from outdoor shops or
Harvey Maps.*

Ordnance Survey

Romsey Road, Maybush, Southampton
SO16 4GU
Customer helpline: 08456 05 05 05
Web: www.ordnancesurvey.gov.uk

*The government mapping agency,
with an enormous range of mapping
products, including of course the
Landranger, Explorer and Outdoor
Leisure series. The free Map Index to
these series can be obtained from the
helpline, and from the web site.
This site also lets you check the precise
coverage of any of the maps in these
series, and you can order on-line.*

Ramblers' Association

2nd Floor, Camelford House,
87-89 Albert Embankment,
London SE1 7BR
Tel: 020 7339 8500
Fax: 020 7339 8501
Web: www.ramblers.org.uk

*Campaigns on behalf of all walkers
for the conservation of countryside,
the upkeep of public paths,
and the freedom to roam. It was a
major influence on the OS in bringing
1:25,000 mapping up to current
standards. The RA publishes
a quarterly magazine and through its
400 local groups offers members a*

BIBLIOGRAPHY

Martin Bagness
"Mountain Navigation for Runners"

This book covers the basic techniques of hill and moorland navigation, but is of particular interest for the many worked examples of route choices, bringing in many factors that are relevant to the hillwalker.

Peter Cliffe
"Mountain Navigation"

A succinct and authoritative account of the techniques and skills required for successful hill navigation.

Wally Keay
"Land Navigation"

Prepared for the Duke of Edinburgh Award, this is a thoroughgoing treatment of the basic skills and techniques for navigating on paths and in the hills, with a slant towards the demands of youth groups.

Eric Langmuir
"Mountaincraft and Leadership"

The 'bible' of outdoor centres, this book covers comprehensively all the skills needed for taking parties on routes in Britain's mountains. There is a detailed chapter on navigation.

Lawrence Latham
"GPS Made Easy"

A well-explained treatment of GPS useage that lets you delve into the subject as little or as far as you want to go.

Martin Moran
"Scotland's Winter Mountains, The Challenges and the Skills"

A personal, passionate and at times enthralling account of bold ventures in the Highlands. The chapter "Navigational Nightmares" brings home the techniques needed to navigate in winter conditions and the difficulties to be faced.

BMC
"Safety on Mountains"

This inexpensive booklet by the British Mountaineering Council provides much sensible advice for the hill walker, giving a grounding on such matters as clothing, equipment, navigation, hazards, first aid, camping, and the environment.

CLIPPY CARDS

These Clippy Cards and Scale Cards have been printed on the following page for you to cut out and use. Best of all mount them on card, trim them carefully to their outlines and take them to an office supplies shop to be encapsulated in plastic. You could get all four in an A5 pouch for encapsulation. Afterwards trim them again, leaving about four millimetres of plastic at the edges.

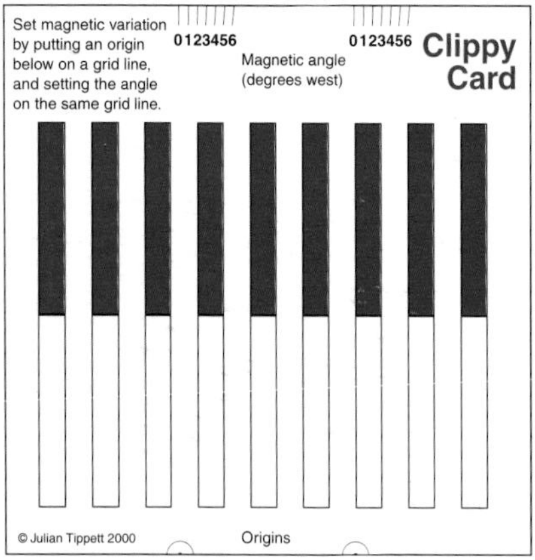

Set magnetic variation
by putting an origin
below on a grid line, **0123456**
and setting the angle
on the same grid line.
Magnetic angle
(degrees west)
0123456
**Clippy
Card**

© Julian Tippett 2000   Origins

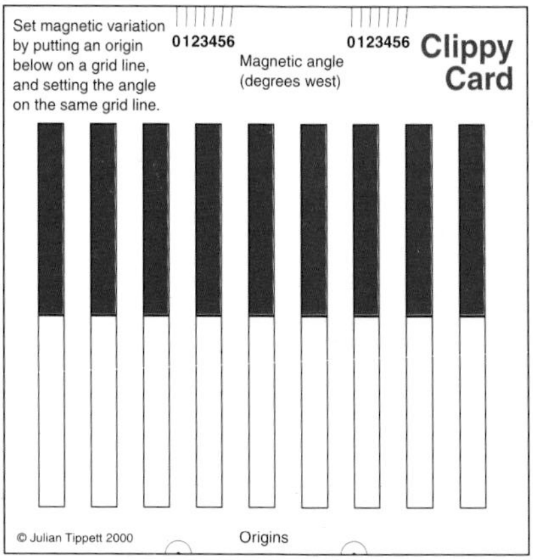

Set magnetic variation
by putting an origin
below on a grid line, **0123456**
and setting the angle
on the same grid line.
Magnetic angle
(degrees west)
0123456
**Clippy
Card**

© Julian Tippett 2000   Origins

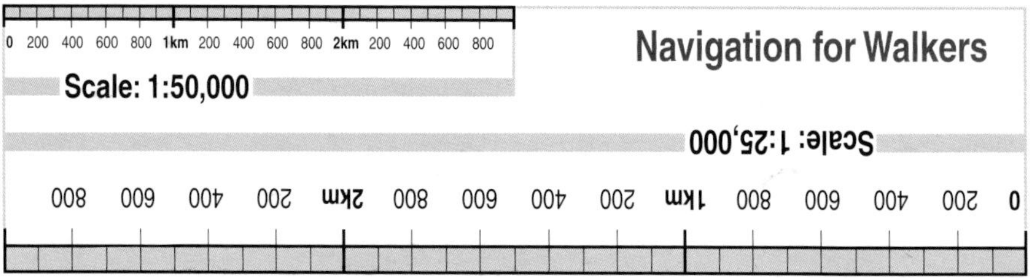

0   200   400   600   800   **1km**   200   400   600   800   **2km**   200   400   600   800

Scale: 1:50,000

Scale: 1:25,000

800   600   400   200   **2km**   800   600   400   200   **1km**   800   600   400   200   **0**

Navigation for Walkers

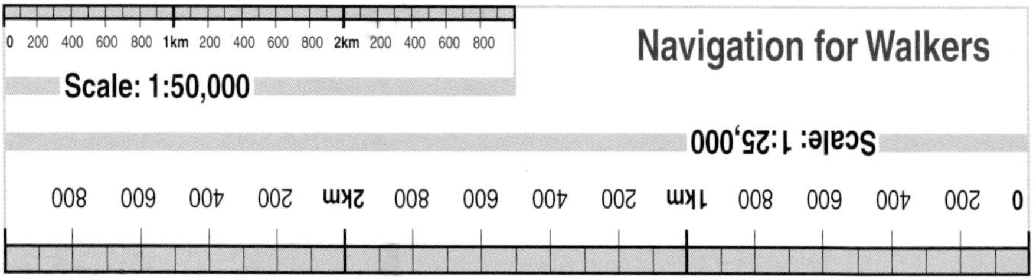

0   200   400   600   800   **1km**   200   400   600   800   **2km**   200   400   600   800

Scale: 1:50,000

Scale: 1:25,000

800   600   400   200   **2km**   800   600   400   200   **1km**   800   600   400   200   **0**

Navigation for Walkers